DAILY SUMMER ACTIVITIES

Content Editing: Jo Ellen Moore
Andrea Weiss
Wendy Zamora
Art Direction: Cheryl Puckett
Cover Design: Liliana Potigian
Illustrators: Len Borozinski
Greg Harris
Jim Palmer
Design/Production: Carolina Caird
Susan Lovell
John D. Williams

EMC 1066

Evan-Moor
EDUCATIONAL PUBLISHERS®
Helping Children Learn since 1979

Congratulations on your purchase of some of the finest teaching materials in the world.

For information about other Evan-Moor products, call 1-800-777-4362, fax 1-800-777-4332, or visit our Web site, www.evan-moor.com. Entire contents © 2012 EVAN-MOOR CORP. 18 Lower Ragsdale Drive, Monterey, CA 93940-5746. Printed in USA.

Contents

Skills	Week 1	2	3	4	5	6	7	8	9	10
Reading Comprehension										
Nonfiction	●	●	●	●	●	●	●	●	●	●
Fiction	●	●		●	●	●	●	●	●	●
Main Idea and Details	●	●	●	●	●	●		●	●	●
Inference	●		●	●	●	●	●	●	●	●
Compare/Contrast				●	●					●
Make Connections	●	●	●	●	●	●	●	●	●	●
Visualization		●				●	●		●	
Sequencing		●			●		●			
Cause and Effect		●		●				●	●	
Fact and Opinion			●							
Prediction			●				●	●		●
Theme	●	●		●		●	●	●	●	●
Character and Setting	●	●		●	●	●			●	●
Grammar/Usage/Mechanics										
Spelling	●	●	●	●	●	●	●	●	●	●
Abbreviation		●	●				●	●	●	
Capitalization	●	●	●	●	●	●	●	●	●	●
Punctuation	●	●	●	●	●	●	●	●	●	●
Possessives		●	●	●		●	●	●		●
Quotation Marks		●		●	●		●	●	●	
Singular/Plural	●	●	●	●		●	●			
Subject/Verb Agreement	●	●	●	●	●			●		
Compound Sentences										●
Syllabification								●		●
Negatives/Double Negatives					●		●	●		
Sentence/Fragment							●			
Independent/Dependent Clauses									●	
Parts of Speech:										
nouns/proper nouns	●			●	●					
verb phrases	●									
present, past, future verbs		●		●		●	●	●	●	
adjectives					●					
pronouns				●	●		●			
adverbs			●			●				
prepositional phrases						●				
conjunctions	●							●		
Vocabulary Development										
Precise Language		●	●							
Idioms	●									
Greek and Latin Word Parts									●	
Base Words			●					●		●

© Evan-Moor Corp. • EMC 1066 • Daily Summer Activities

Skills	Week 1	2	3	4	5	6	7	8	9	10
Vocabulary Development (continued)										
Prefixes								●		
Suffixes										●
Homophones				●						●
Homographs							●			
Blended Words									●	
Compound Words					●					
Synonyms									●	
Antonyms						●				●
Clipped Words						●				
Math										
Addition	●		●	●	●				●	
Subtraction	●				●					
Multiplication	●		●	●		●	●	●		
Division		●	●	●		●		●		
Word Problems	●	●	●	●	●	●	●		●	●
Place Value	●			●						
Greater Than/Less Than/Equal to									●	
Fractions				●			●	●		
Function Tables				●						
Using Graphs/Tables/Charts		●					●	●		
Ordered Pairs on a Graph										●
Measurement:										
units of measurement					●	●				
linear								●		
volume				●						
perimeter	●									
Decimals/Percents		●			●	●		●	●	●
Polygons	●									●
Range/Mean/Median/Mode									●	
Geography										
Physical Maps	●						●	●		
Political Maps	●		●	●		●	●	●	●	●
Latitude and Longitude		●								
Road Maps				●			●			
Product Maps					●					
Map Grids						●				
Legends	●			●		●	●	●	●	●
Projection Maps										
Compass Rose/Directions	●		●		●	●	●	●	●	●
Thinking Skills										
Riddles/Problem Solving	●	●	●	●	●	●	●	●	●	●

© Evan-Moor Corp. • EMC 1066 • Daily Summer Activities

About This Book

What's in It

Ten Weekly Sections

Each of the 10 weekly sections contains half- and full-page activities in several subject areas, including math, geography, reading comprehension, spelling, grammar, vocabulary, and critical thinking. The practice sessions are short, giving your child a review of what was learned during the previous school year.

Each week, your child will complete the following:

Read It!	2 comprehension activities consisting of a fiction or nonfiction reading passage and 4 multiple-choice questions
Spell It	1 spelling activity practicing the week's 12 spelling words
Language Lines	2 language arts activities practicing a variety of grammar and usage skills
Write It Right	1 editing activity to correct errors in spelling, grammar, and punctuation
Vocabulary	1 activity for building vocabulary and practicing such skills as compound words, word parts, synonyms, and homographs
Math Time	3 math activities on skills including word problems, fractions, and measurement
Geography	1 map activity testing basic geography concepts
In My Own Words	2 creative-writing exercises
Mind Jigglers	1 critical-thinking activity
Weekly Record Form	a place to record the most memorable moment of the week, as well as a reading log for recording the number of minutes spent reading each day

© Evan-Moor Corp. • EMC 1066 • Daily Summer Activities

How to Use It

The short practice sessions in *Daily Summer Activities* act as a bridge between grades, preparing your child for the coming school year by keeping him or her fresh on the concepts and skills mastered this past year. After completing the book, your child will feel more confident as he or she progresses to the next grade. You can help by following the suggestions below to ensure your child's success.

Provide Time and Space

Make sure that your child has a quiet place for completing the activities. The practice session should be short and successful. Consider your child's personality and other activities as you decide how and where to schedule daily practice periods.

Provide Encouragement and Support

Your response is important to your child's feelings of success. Keep your remarks positive and recognize the effort your child has made. Correct mistakes together. Work toward independence, guiding practice when necessary.

Check In Each Week

Use the weekly record sheet to talk about the most memorable moments and learning experiences of the week and to discuss the literature your child is reading.

Be a Model Reader

The most important thing you can do is to make sure your child sees *you* reading. Read books, magazines, and newspapers. Visit libraries and bookstores. Point out interesting signs, maps, and advertisements wherever you go. Even though your child is an independent reader, you can still share the reading experience by discussing what you read every day.

Go on Learning Excursions

Learning takes place everywhere and through many kinds of experiences. Build learning power over the summer by:

➤ visiting local museums and historic sites. Use a guide book or search online to find points of interest in your area. The Chamber of Commerce and AAA are good sources of information about local attractions.

➤ collecting art materials and working together to create a collage, mobile, or scrapbook.

➤ going to a play, concert, or other show at a local theater or performance center.

➤ creating a movie of your child's favorite story. Write a simple script, make basic costumes and props, and recruit friends and family members to be the actors. Practice until everyone is comfortable before shooting the video.

➤ planting a garden. If you are short on space, plant in containers.

Spell It

This list contains all of the weekly spelling words practiced in the book.

A
action
afraid
agriculture
allow
already
amphibian
answer
appreciate
atmosphere
attendance
autobiography
automatic

B
bicycle
biography
biology
briefly
business

C
calendar
carried
certain
characteristic
chew
choose
civilization
committee
cough
cue
currency
cyclone

D
daybreak
design
discipline
doubt

E
early
earth
eighth
embarrass
enact
enough
environment
exaggerate
exciting
existing
explain

F
favorite
finished
flu
foreign
fountain
fourth
fragile

G
geology
gloomy
grammar
graph

H
honor

I
intersection
island

K
knapsack
knowledge

L
limb
listen
loneliest
loose

M
mayor
mischief
musician

N
necessary
nephew

O
occasion

P
payment
pearl
pharmacy
photograph
physical
portable
principle
purpose

Q
quickest

R
radio
receive
relieve
representative
rhythm
roughest
route
ruin

S
semicircle
separate
sincerely
skiing
sleigh
smuggler
staff
station
straight
studied
substitute
succeed
surrounded
swimming

T
talking
they
thirsty
thorough
threw
tiniest
trading
transport
traveler
triumph
trouble
truth
Tuesday

U
urgent
usually

W
weigh
whistle
wonder
wrestle

WEEK 1

Check off each box as you complete the day's work.

Spelling Words

afraid

daybreak

eighth

explain

favorite

payment

radio

sleigh

station

straight

they

weigh

Get Creative!

Turn this scribble into a face.

A Memorable Moment

What sticks in your mind about this week? Write about it.

_____

_____

_____

_____

_____

_____

Reading Record

	Book Title	Pages	Time
Monday			
Tuesday			
Wednesday			
Thursday			
Friday			

Describe a character you read about this week.

_____

_____

_____

_____

_____

Read the article. Then answer the questions.

Hurricane Plane

You might know that wind vanes tell you which way the wind is blowing and that thermometers tell you how hot or cold it is outside. But did you know that airplanes can be used to study hurricanes?

On November 1, 2007, an aircraft flew through a dangerous hurricane. People on the ground controlled the plane, so nobody was inside it. However, it was full of equipment used to take pictures and record data as the plane passed through the storm.

While large planes can safely fly over a hurricane, looking at a hurricane from above doesn't tell scientists everything they want to know. This is because most hurricanes get their energy from warm water in the ocean. Scientists wanted to learn more about what happens where that warm ocean water meets the air in a hurricane. So, they sent in the small remote-controlled plane. The plane studied how clouds form and measured the temperature of the air and water. It also recorded many images of the storm.

Scientists are still studying the information they collected using the plane. Many hope it will help them better understand how hurricanes form and move so that people can be better prepared when a hurricane comes.

· ·

1. **When did scientists use the hurricane plane?**

   Ⓐ in spring

   Ⓑ during summer

   Ⓒ in fall

   Ⓓ during winter

2. **What is one lesson from the passage?**

   Ⓐ Gathering information safely is more important than risking lives.

   Ⓑ Hurricanes are more important than airplanes.

   Ⓒ Using equipment to gather information is more important than using scientists.

   Ⓓ Airplanes are more important than thermometers.

3. **Why did scientists need a plane that could fly through a hurricane?**

   Ⓐ They were afraid to fly above the hurricane.

   Ⓑ They wanted to be closer to where the air meets the water.

   Ⓒ The hurricane was in their way.

   Ⓓ They did not have a plane that could fly higher than a hurricane.

4. **How do you think the scientists felt when the plane flew through the hurricane?**

   Ⓐ disappointed

   Ⓑ angry

   Ⓒ silly

   Ⓓ proud

Write It Right

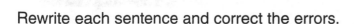

Rewrite each sentence and correct the errors.

1. i red a amazing story abut the hardships of sum early travelers

   _____

2. we needs to be at the airport by 945 or well miss hour flight

   _____

3. sarah can run faster then anyone i no

   _____

4. peter and shawn walks to the busstop at seven oclock

   _____

MATH TIME

What place value does the numeral **3** hold in each number? The first one has been done for you.

1. 135 _____tens_____

2. 394 _____

3. 1,293 _____

4. 93,649 _____

5. 320,196 _____

6. 5,462,349 _____

7. 194,634 _____

8. 3,579,216 _____

9. 2,634,912 _____

10. 9,616,493 _____

SPELL IT

Fill in the missing letter or letters to make the spelling words for this week.

1. p _____ ment

2. w _____

3. f _____ vorite

4. afr _____ d

5. d _____ br _____ k

6. sl _____

7. _____ th

8. str _____ ght

9. expl _____ n

10. th _____

11. st _____ tion

12. r _____ dio

In My Own Words

Imagine that your pet could talk. Write about what it might say.

LANGUAGE LINES

A noun names a person, place, thing, or idea.

Write each noun in the correct category.

flag	plow	colony
horse	leader	change
inventor	progress	pioneer
independence	wilderness	laboratory

person

_____

_____

_____

place

_____

_____

_____

thing

_____

_____

_____

idea

_____

_____

_____

MATH TIME

Calculate the answer. If the answer is an *odd* number, circle it in green.
If it is an *even* number, underline it in red.

34	29	46	83	91	52	77	90
+ 26	+ 45	+ 13	+ 74	+ 49	+ 28	+ 36	+ 88

61	37	85	27	76	16	98	14
+ 82	+ 29	+ 48	+ 19	+ 79	+ 46	+ 23	+ 37

94	16	69	37	21	48	80	55
+ 17	+ 89	+ 34	+ 81	+ 60	+ 78	+ 47	+ 68

© Evan-Moor Corp. • EMC 1066 • Daily Summer Activities

Read the story. Then answer the questions.

The Amazing Rowlands

Greg Rowland sat in the living room, feeling miserable. His father was a famous magician. His mother was an expert archer and acrobat. And his older sisters were lion tamers. Everyone in Greg's family was amazing, except for Greg. The most exciting thing he could do was to make grilled cheese sandwiches.

"Why so glum?" his mother asked, walking into the living room on her hands.

"I feel very un-amazing," Greg said.

"That's silly," said Greg's father, who appeared in the room in a puff of purple smoke. "You're the most amazing Rowland of all!"

"That's impossible," Greg said. "I can't do magic, I roll sideways whenever I try a somersault, and I'm not brave enough to pet a kitten, much less a lion."

"Yes, but who helps me practice my new tricks?" Dad asked. "And who points out when I make a mistake or when people can see the rabbit wriggling under my hat?"

"And who makes sure my bow and arrows are all in good shape?" asked Mom.

"And who helps us clean out the lions' cages?" called Greg's sisters from the kitchen.

Greg's mother rolled into a sitting position on the floor beside him and ruffled his hair. "You don't have to be flashy to be amazing, son," she said.

. . . .

1. **What is the lesson of the story?**
   - Ⓐ Appearances can be deceiving.
   - Ⓑ People cannot change who they are.
   - Ⓒ Sometimes greatness is not easily seen.
   - Ⓓ Trust in people's actions, not their words.

2. **Which of these best describes Greg?**
   - Ⓐ helpful
   - Ⓑ brave
   - Ⓒ unkind
   - Ⓓ grateful

3. **Why does Greg feel bad?**
   - Ⓐ He does not appreciate his family.
   - Ⓑ He does not think he has talent.
   - Ⓒ He is tired of helping others.
   - Ⓓ He wishes his family were more normal.

4. **Where does the story take place?**
   - Ⓐ at the circus
   - Ⓑ near a lion's cage
   - Ⓒ in Greg's room
   - Ⓓ in the Rowland home

Vo·cab·u·lar·y

An **idiom** is a phrase that means something different from what its individual words seem to mean. Idioms are often funny or colorful expressions.

Idiom: Who let the cat out of the bag?

What it means: "Who told the secret or ruined the surprise?"
What it does *not* mean: "Who allowed a captured cat to escape?"

A. Write the letter of each underlined idiom's meaning.

_____ 1. Don't <u>make a mountain out of a molehill</u>.

_____ 2. I'll be at the party with <u>bells on</u>.

_____ 3. <u>It rubs me the wrong way</u> when you call me "kiddo."

_____ 4. In restaurants, my little cousin is <u>like a bull in a china shop</u>.

_____ 5. <u>A little birdie told me</u> that you're mad at me. Is that true?

_____ 6. When my mom lost her job, she was <u>down in the dumps</u>.

_____ 7. Pablo is <u>a night owl</u>, so he often stays up late reading.

_____ 8. When everyone yelled "Surprise!" <u>you could have knocked me over with a feather</u>.

a. irritates me

b. a person whose name I won't mention

c. very likely to break things or cause a mess

d. to exaggerate so as to make a slight matter seem like a big deal

e. a person who likes to stay up late

f. feeling sad and depressed

g. I was extremely surprised and shocked.

h. in a happy mood and ready to celebrate

B. Write a sentence using an idiom from Activity A.

_____

_____

LANGUAGE LINES

In some sentences, a main verb and a helping verb form a **verb phrase**. The **main verb** shows action and the **helping verb** expresses something more about action.

verb phrase

Maria can take a taxi to the airport.

helping verb   main verb

can   take

Underline the verb phrase. Write the helping verb and the main verb in the correct column. The first one has been done for you.

Verb Phrase	Helping Verb	Main Verb
1. Everyone at the airport is hurrying.	is	hurrying
2. The lines at the counter are getting longer.		
3. I have slipped our tickets into this envelope.		
4. I must remember that!		
5. Everyone will board the plane soon.		
6. The plane is lifting off the runway.		
7. I can see our house from here.		

In My Own Words

Write a description of your favorite ice-cream flavor.

Mind Jigglers

At the Ice-Cream Store

A. Write a sentence using the words *ice cream*, *paid*, *hot fudge*, and *baseball*.

_____

_____

_____

1	ABC 2	DEF 3
GHI 4	JKL 5	MNO 6
PRUS 7	TUV 8	WXYZ 9
*	0	#

B. Use the phone keypad to decode the ice-cream flavors. Remember, numbers **2** through **9** can represent one of three or four different letters. **Example: 243779 = CHERRY**

8264552 _____

282253   486 _____

76259   7623 _____

7872923779 _____

246265283   2447 _____

C. Jim owns an ice-cream store. Use the clues to find out how many ice-cream cones he sold last week.

- He sold more than 300 but fewer than 350.

- The last digit is an odd number.

- The second digit is 3 less than the last digit.

- The sum of the first 2 digits equals the last digit.

- The sum of all digits is 14.

Jim has sold _____ ice-cream cones.

D. Everybody is talking about Jim's new ice-cream flavor, Chocolate Dream. Each day, his sales for this flavor have tripled! How many scoops did Jim sell each day?

Monday: 1 scoop

Tuesday: _____ scoops

Wednesday: _____ scoops

Thursday: _____ scoops

Friday: _____ scoops

Saturday: _____ scoops!

© Evan-Moor Corp. • EMC 1066 • Daily Summer Activities

Solve the Tongue Twister

A. Find the perimeter of each polygon. Write it on the line next to the letter, which you will use in Activity B. The first one has been done for you.

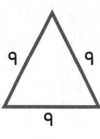

9 9
9

__27__ = **c**

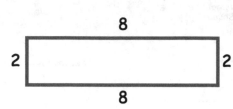

8
2   2
8

_____ = **d**

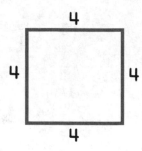

4
4   4
4

_____ = **e**

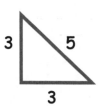

3   5
3

_____ = **g**

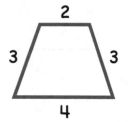

2
3   3
4

_____ = **i**

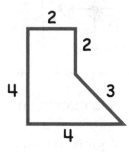

2
2
4   3
4

_____ = **k**

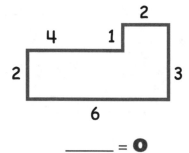

2
4   1
2   3
6

_____ = **o**

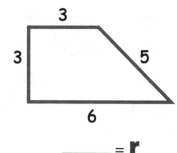

3
3   5
6

_____ = **r**

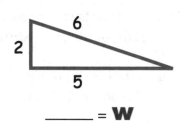

6
2
5

_____ = **w**

B. Fill in the puzzle with the letters from Activity A that match the numbers below. The letters will spell out a tongue twister. How many times can you say it in ten seconds?

| 17 | 12 | 11 | 12 | 20 | | 13 | 12 | C 27 | 15 | 16 | 17 |

| 17 | 18 | 27 | 15 | 16 | 17 |

Geography

Washington State

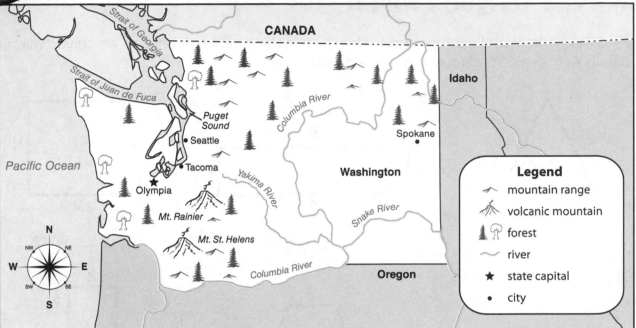

Use the map to answer the questions.

1. What is the capital of Washington? _____

2. How many volcanoes are shown on the map of Washington? Name them.

   _____

3. Do forests cover less than one-fourth, more than _____
   half, or all of Washington?

4. What is the name of the river that helps form _____
   the border between Washington and Oregon?

5. What route would a ship traveling from the Pacific Ocean to the port of Seattle take?

   _____

   _____

6. Name all the states and countries that border Washington.

   _____

WEEK 2

Check off each box as you complete the day's work.

Spelling Words

chew

choose

cue

flu

gloomy

loose

route

ruin

threw

truth

Tuesday

usually

Get Creative!

Draw a picture to match the caption below.

"Now *that's* a pizza!"

A Memorable Moment

What sticks in your mind about this week? Write about it.

_____

_____

_____

_____

_____

_____

Reading Record

	Book Title	Pages	Time
Monday	_____	_____	_____
Tuesday	_____	_____	_____
Wednesday	_____	_____	_____
Thursday	_____	_____	_____
Friday	_____	_____	_____

Describe a character you read about this week.

_____

_____

_____

_____

_____

_____

22

Read the story. Then answer the questions.

Wendy's Walk

Wendy was hot, tired, and bored. She trudged along behind her brother, Bill, as they hiked up the steep trail to the cabin at the fire lookout tower. Buzzards circled lazily in the sky above them, and Wendy wondered whether they would eat her bones if she died out here. The sun was blazing hot, the trees and bushes were ugly, and the hike was boring.

"Almost there!" Bill said cheerily. This was his first summer working as a fire spotter at the state park. He would be staying on top of a mountain all summer, watching for fires in the forest. He was excited and had not noticed how tired Wendy had become.

Finally, Wendy couldn't take another step unless she rested first. She sat in the shade of a tall pine tree and drank lemonade from her canteen. Bill continued on for a few more moments before realizing that Wendy was no longer behind him.

"Sorry," he said, returning and sitting beside his sister. "I forgot your legs are shorter than mine."

Wendy stuck her tongue out at her brother but then quickly smiled when he handed her some dried strawberries and peanuts from his backpack.

"If you chew them together, it's like making a peanut butter and jelly sandwich in your mouth," he said.

The strawberries and peanuts tasted delicious. Wendy closed her eyes, stretched her arms and legs, and wiggled her toes in her hiking boots. She heard a songbird twittering in a nearby bush and caught the smell of wildflowers. Suddenly the sun didn't seem so hot, and the trees weren't as ugly anymore.

· ·

1. **Where does the story take place?**

   Ⓐ in a fire lookout cabin

   Ⓑ in Wendy and Bill's backyard

   Ⓒ at a state park

   Ⓓ in a forest during a wildfire

2. **Which of these best describes what happens to Wendy by the end of the passage?**

   Ⓐ She has a better attitude about the hike.

   Ⓑ She is ready to go home.

   Ⓒ She decides to become a fire spotter.

   Ⓓ She thinks her brother is mean.

3. **Which of these best describes Bill?**

   Ⓐ He does not care about his sister.

   Ⓑ He is happy and eager to start his job.

   Ⓒ He does not enjoy hiking with his family.

   Ⓓ He does not like Wendy's behavior.

4. **When does the story take place?**

   Ⓐ in early spring

   Ⓑ in late summer

   Ⓒ in winter

   Ⓓ in early summer

Write It Right

Rewrite each sentence and correct the errors.

1. please put a ice cube in there lemonade

   _____

2. does the music start at 400 or 430 inquired Ms Clark

   _____

3. the workmen has come to repair the roof on hermans house

   _____

4. wood you put these groceries away emily her mom asked

   _____

MATH TIME

Complete the division problems. Note the remainder when appropriate.

$4\overline{)24}$ $4\overline{)32}$ $5\overline{)49}$ $9\overline{)58}$ $8\overline{)29}$

$2\overline{)15}$ $5\overline{)84}$ $6\overline{)35}$ $8\overline{)27}$ $2\overline{)23}$

$7\overline{)25}$ $8\overline{)62}$ $4\overline{)20}$ $6\overline{)42}$ $5\overline{)81}$

SPELL IT

The sound of /oo/, as in **food**, is spelled many ways:

oo   ou   ue   u   ew

Which spelling words for this week have about the same meaning as these words? Write the spelling words on the line. Then circle the letters that stand for the /oo/ sound in each word.

1. dreary: _____

2. pathway: _____

3. honesty: _____

4. select: _____

5. baggy: _____

6. crush with teeth: _____

7. hint: _____

8. tossed: _____

9. destroy: _____

10. day after Monday: _____

11. regularly: _____

12. kind of illness: _____

In My Own Words

Which would you rather be, a porcupine or a skunk? Why?

Mind Jigglers

Picture This

Write the familiar phrase that each clue illustrates. The first one is done for you.

JACK Jack in the box _____	the **weather** I'm _____ _____	SIT**ME** _____ _____
My cat **WEIGHT** _____ _____	A dayday day day day day day**WEEK** _____ _____	egg egg egg egg egg egg egg egg egg egg egg egg _____ _____
right **THERE** _____ _____	the **BRIDGE** water _____ _____	a t i ① BUSH u g g _____ _____
🌲 🍎 **CAKE** (reversed) _____ _____	h a n g i n g (in circle) _____ _____	The cow jumped the moon _____ _____

Fruit Pie

Read the pie chart below. Next, answer the questions using the chart on the right. Then write the letter of the correct answer next to the question. The letters will spell out the name of a popular fruit drink.

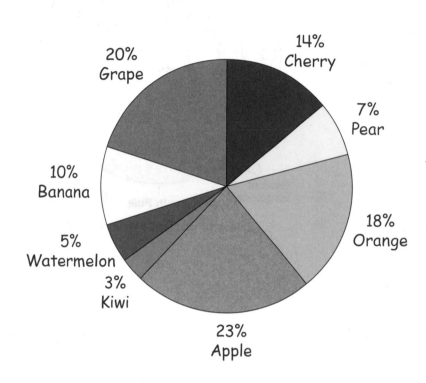

14% Cherry

7% Pear

18% Orange

23% Apple

3% Kiwi

5% Watermelon

10% Banana

20% Grape

Cherry = **E**	
Pear = **O**	
Orange = **E**	
Apple = **A**	
Kiwi = **M**	
Watermelon = **D**	
Banana = **L**	
Grape = **N**	

_____ What fruit did only 10% of people list as their favorite?

_____ What fruit did 14% list as their favorite?

_____ What fruit was the least favorite?

_____ What fruit did half as many list as their favorite compared to cherry?

_____ What fruit is shown as the second most favorite kind?

_____ What fruit was the most popular?

_____ What fruit did half as many list as their favorite compared to banana?

_____ What fruit did 18% of people list as their favorite?

A Memorable Moment

What sticks in your mind about this week? Write about it.

_____

_____

_____

_____

_____

_____

Reading Record

	Book Title	Pages	Time
Monday	_____	_____	_____
Tuesday	_____	_____	_____
Wednesday	_____	_____	_____
Thursday	_____	_____	_____
Friday	_____	_____	_____

Describe a character you read about this week.

_____

_____

_____

_____

_____

Read the article. Then answer the questions.

Brain Freeze

Have you ever eaten ice cream on a hot day and suddenly felt a sharp pain in your head? If so, you have had a very common experience that some people call a "brain freeze."

Brain freezes are caused when cold food or liquid touches the roof of your mouth. Nerves in your mouth send a signal to your brain. Your brain then turns the signal into a sharp pain. However, the pain does not go to your mouth where the cold is—it stays in your head.

Most brain freezes last for less than 30 seconds. But if you want to make it go away quicker, you can try a couple of tricks. When you start to get a brain freeze, push your tongue against the roof of your mouth. This sometimes warms up your mouth so that the nerves don't send the signal that causes a headache. You can also try preventing brain freeze from the start by eating and drinking more slowly. If you take smaller bites or sips and wait longer between them, your mouth won't get as cold. Of course, sometimes a cold drink or an ice-cream cone on a hot day is just too good to enjoy slowly!

· ·

1. **What causes a brain freeze?**

   Ⓐ eating too much ice cream or cold food

   Ⓑ eating something cold and then something warm

   Ⓒ cold food or drink touching the roof of your mouth

   Ⓓ eating cold food on very hot days

2. **According to the passage, which of these is a way to cure a brain freeze?**

   Ⓐ putting something warm on your tongue

   Ⓑ placing your tongue on the roof of your mouth

   Ⓒ eating cold things more quickly

   Ⓓ eating warm and cold foods together

3. **Why does eating or drinking slowly help prevent brain freezes?**

   Ⓐ Your mouth does not get as cold.

   Ⓑ Your brain cannot recognize what you are eating or drinking.

   Ⓒ The thing you are eating or drinking does not touch your tongue.

   Ⓓ The brain freeze does not last as long.

4. **Which of these would probably *not* cause a brain freeze?**

   Ⓐ gulping down a glass of cold lemonade

   Ⓑ eating an ice-cream cone quickly before it melts

   Ⓒ chewing a lot of ice

   Ⓓ slowly sipping a glass of iced tea

Write It Right

Rewrite each sentence and correct the errors.

1. mavis ate most of her salad but she left a orange slice

   _____

2. dr conrads wife jill will join him at the ceremony

   _____

3. was the musicians nervous before the concert begun

   _____

4. mr matthews told jake that he shuld go to the principles office

   _____

MATH TIME

Complete the problems. Two of them have been done for you.

$\frac{4}{5} + \frac{1}{5}$ = ___$\frac{5}{5} = 1$___

$3\frac{1}{3} + 1\frac{2}{3}$ = _____

$3\frac{3}{4} + 1\frac{3}{4}$ = _____

$1\frac{1}{2} + 3\frac{1}{4}$ = _____

$2\frac{1}{5} + 3\frac{1}{2}$ = _____

$3\frac{4}{5} + 5\frac{1}{3}$ = _____

$\frac{5}{8} + \frac{1}{8}$ = _____

$5\frac{2}{3} + 2\frac{1}{3}$ = ___$\frac{17}{3} + \frac{7}{3} = \frac{24}{3} = 8$___

$4 + \frac{1}{4}$ = _____

$3\frac{1}{3} + \frac{2}{3}$ = _____

$3\frac{1}{3} + 1\frac{3}{4}$ = _____

$4\frac{2}{5} + 1\frac{4}{5}$ = _____

SPELL IT

Add the ending to each base word to correctly write the spelling words for the week. Remember that the spelling of some words will change when the endings are added.

Add –*ing*	Add –*ed*	Add –*est*
ski _____	study _____	quick _____
excite _____	carry _____	tiny _____
exist _____	surround _____	lonely _____
trade _____	finish _____	
swim _____		

In My Own Words

Imagine you had a swimming pool full of jelly. What would you do with it? Be creative.

LANGUAGE LINES

Adverbs modify verbs, adjectives, and other adverbs.
Adverbs can tell when, where, and how something is happening.

A. Circle the adverb in each sentence.

1. Soon we arrived at the aquarium.

2. We clapped and cheered loudly.

3. Someone was waiting for us outside.

4. We eagerly left the bus.

B. Does the underlined adverb tell *when, where,* or *how*? Circle the correct answer.

1. We <u>excitedly</u> walked to the entrance.	**when**	**where**	**how**
2. The otters swam <u>nearby</u>.	**when**	**where**	**how**
3. A guide <u>quietly</u> talked to us about otters.	**when**	**where**	**how**
4. <u>Then</u> it was feeding time.	**when**	**where**	**how**
5. The otters waited <u>patiently</u> for their supper.	**when**	**where**	**how**

MATH TIME

Solve the word problems about recycling.

1. Tim's family was collecting aluminum cans to recycle. They found out that they would get two cents for every three cans they collected. If they collected 2,187 cans, how much money did they receive?

   Answer: _____

2. Bettler Elementary School was recycling their paper. They found that when they filled a barrel with paper, it weighed an average of 463 pounds. If they collected 16 barrels of paper during the year, what was the approximate weight of the paper?

   Answer: _____

Read one person's opinion of Lake Tahoe.
Then answer the questions.

The Lake on Top of a Mountain

Imagine a lake as blue as the summer sky, surrounded by thousands of pine trees and towering mountains. It sounds like something from a storybook, but Lake Tahoe is a real place in the Sierra Nevada mountains, along the border of California and Nevada.

People come during every season to enjoy Lake Tahoe. It is the perfect spot for camping, boating, fishing, biking, and hiking. However, Lake Tahoe is best known for its snow sports. Most of the small towns surrounding Lake Tahoe have lodges where families can go to ski or snowboard. These resorts are much more fun to stay at than the ones in other parts of the country.

Thousands of people visit Lake Tahoe each year, but the area was popular long before California and Nevada were even states. Native Americans from the Washoe (WASH-oh) tribe traveled through the mountains and spent their summers at Lake Tahoe. In fact, the name *Tahoe* comes from a Washoe word meaning "big water." The Washoe were expert hunters who used the land and water for their food supply. They even created many legends about the lake. The best one is about a giant birdlike monster that lived in the middle of the lake and ate people!

While people now use Lake Tahoe mostly for fun rather than survival, it is still important to keep the water and land clean. California and Nevada work together to make sure these natural resources are used wisely. It would be terrible if the lake and mountains became too polluted for everyone to enjoy. There is no place as beautiful or fun for a vacation as Lake Tahoe.

....

1. **Which one is an opinion about the ski resorts in Lake Tahoe?**

   Ⓐ They are more fun than other ski resorts.

   Ⓑ Many towns around the lake have resorts.

   Ⓒ The resorts are popular during the winter.

   Ⓓ Families can stay at the resorts.

2. **Which one of these is an opinion?**

   Ⓐ The Washoe tribe spent summers at Lake Tahoe.

   Ⓑ It would be terrible if Lake Tahoe became too dirty for people to enjoy.

   Ⓒ People come to fish on Lake Tahoe.

   Ⓓ Lake Tahoe is surrounded by pine trees.

3. **Which one is a fact about Lake Tahoe?**

   Ⓐ It is a perfect spot for camping.

   Ⓑ Its resorts are fun to stay at.

   Ⓒ It is better for snow sports than water sports.

   Ⓓ It borders California and Nevada.

4. **Which one is an opinion about the Washoe?**

   Ⓐ They created many legends.

   Ⓑ They hunted for their food.

   Ⓒ They traveled through the mountains.

   Ⓓ Their best legend is about a bird monster.

Vo·cab·u·lar·y

Use the clues to help fill in the blanks and circles. Only the circled letters should change from one word to the next. The first three have been done for you.

1. a tree branch   l   i   m   b

2. a green citrus fruit   l   i   m   (e)

3. seconds, minutes, hours, and so on   (t)   i   m   e

4. an antonym for *wild*   __ ◯ __ __

5. what celebrities have   ◯ __ __ __

6. not real   __ __ ◯ __

7. to create   ◯ __ __ __

8. a husband or wife   __ __ ◯ __

9. an antonym for *female*   __ __ ◯ __

10. driving 60 _____s per hour   __ ◯ __ __

11. a square piece on a floor   ◯ __ __ __

12. a story   __ ◯ __ __

13. an antonym for *short*   __ __ __ ◯

14. a shopping center   ◯ __ __ __

15. a factory that makes flour or lumber   __ ◯ __ __

16. Jack's water-fetching partner (Jack and __)   ◯ __ __ __

17. might take one if you're sick   ◯ __ __ __

18. to yank or drag   __ ◯ __ __

LANGUAGE LINES

Can and **may** are often confused. **Can** means
"to be able to," while **may** means "allowed to."

Write *can* or *may* to complete each sentence correctly.

1. Emily and Yuko _____ both run very fast.

2. "_____ I run with you?" asked David.

3. "How fast _____ you run?" asked Yuko.

4. "I _____ run pretty fast," David replied.

5. "You _____ run with us this afternoon," Emily said.

6. "That way, we _____ see if we are good running buddies," said Yuko.

7. David showed that he _____ run as fast as Emily and Yuko.

8. They told him that he _____ run with them anytime.

In My Own Words

List 10 things you want to do when you are an adult.

Mind Jigglers

Hink Pinks

Hink Pinks are rhyming words that are the answers to clues. For example, an *obese feline* is a *fat cat.* See if you can identify these other hink pinks.

1. an unhappy father: _____

2. a funny, young female horse: _____

3. an uncovered seat: _____

4. a contest with fire: _____

5. a hog dance: _____

6. a loyal color: _____

7. not a real cobra: _____

8. a frog relative on the highway: _____

9. a library burglar: _____

10. 24 hours of games: _____

11. a twisted penny: _____

12. an intelligent body organ: _____

13. an orca prison: _____

14. a hilarious rabbit: _____

15. 50 percent of a giggle: _____

16. an ill young chicken: _____

MATH TIME

Write the quotient below each problem. Then color each square as directed in the chart at the bottom.

18 ÷ 2	6 ÷ 1	60 ÷ 10	16 ÷ 2	12 ÷ 2	54 ÷ 9	54 ÷ 6
18 ÷ 3	99 ÷ 11	14 ÷ 2	70 ÷ 10	21 ÷ 3	81 ÷ 9	12 ÷ 3
66 ÷ 11	63 ÷ 9	27 ÷ 3	48 ÷ 6	63 ÷ 7	28 ÷ 4	48 ÷ 8
32 ÷ 4	14 ÷ 2	64 ÷ 8	25 ÷ 5	56 ÷ 7	77 ÷ 11	24 ÷ 3
24 ÷ 4	56 ÷ 8	9 ÷ 1	80 ÷ 10	36 ÷ 4	35 ÷ 5	8 ÷ 2
40 ÷ 10	18 ÷ 2	49 ÷ 7	7 ÷ 1	42 ÷ 6	72 ÷ 8	42 ÷ 7
90 ÷ 10	30 ÷ 5	44 ÷ 11	40 ÷ 5	36 ÷ 6	16 ÷ 4	45 ÷ 5

Quotient	Color
9	yellow
8	red
7	green
6 or 4	blue
5	your choice

Geography

United States: North-Central Region

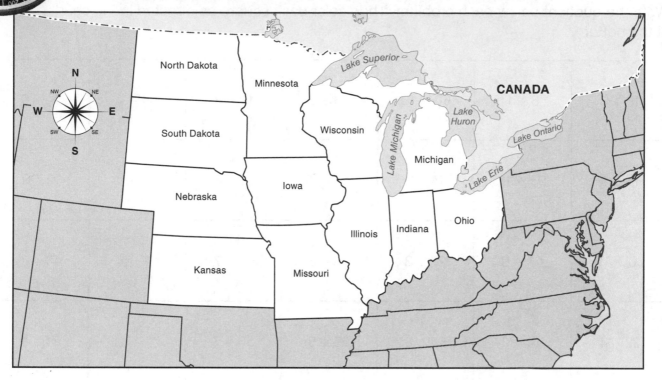

Use the map to answer the questions.

1. How many states are in this region? _____

2. How many states on the map border at least one of the Great Lakes? _____

3. What country is north of this region? _____

4. Which state is directly west of Lake Superior? _____

5. Which state is south of Lake Erie? _____

6. Name the four westernmost states of the region.

_____

West of Greenwich   Longitude West of Greenwich

120°   B   150°   C   180°   D   150°   E   120°   F   90°

© Evan-Moor Corp. MC 1066

WEEK 4

Check off each box as you complete the day's work.

Spelling Words

calendar

certain

early

earth

grammar

mayor

pearl

purpose

smuggler

thirsty

urgent

wonder

Get Creative!

Draw a hat that could win the World's Silliest Hat Contest.

A Memorable Moment

What sticks in your mind about this week? Write about it.

_____

_____

_____

_____

_____

_____

Reading Record

	Book Title	Pages	Time
Monday	_____	_____	_____
Tuesday	_____	_____	_____
Wednesday	_____	_____	_____
Thursday	_____	_____	_____
Friday	_____	_____	_____

Describe a character you read about this week.

_____

_____

_____

_____

_____

46

Read the story. Then answer the questions.

The Boulder and the King

There was once a wise king who was ready to stop being the king. So he ordered some workers to roll a large boulder onto the road that led through town. Then the king hid nearby and watched to see if anyone would move the huge rock from its place in the road. This person would become king.

The first man to pass by was the city's wealthiest person. He bitterly complained that he was too rich to have a boulder in his way. As he walked around the boulder, he shouted, "I must let the king know how angry I am!"

Soon the town's smartest person came to the boulder in the road. She complained loudly that the king should do a better job of keeping the roads clear. Then she, too, walked around the boulder.

Finally, a farmer came along, carrying a load of vegetables. As soon as he arrived at the boulder, he set down his vegetables and tried to move the rock. "Other people might need to use this road," the farmer said to himself. "If I can move it, then I should do so."

After much hard work, the farmer finally succeeded in rolling the boulder off the road. He then noticed a hole where the boulder had been. Inside the hole was a box. The farmer opened the box to find the king's crown and a note. The note read, "For your hard work and for caring about others, you are now the king!"

. . . .

1. **What is one theme of the story?**

   Ⓐ Being rich is better than being wise.

   Ⓑ By taking time to help others, you may help yourself.

   Ⓒ Farmers often make the best leaders.

   Ⓓ Being rewarded makes a job less meaningful.

2. **The wise king wanted the next king to be _____.**

   Ⓐ wealthy instead of poor

   Ⓑ smart instead of rich

   Ⓒ a farmer instead of a merchant

   Ⓓ a hard worker instead of a complainer

3. **Which statement might the farmer most agree with?**

   Ⓐ Working hard has few rewards.

   Ⓑ Complaining will get you noticed.

   Ⓒ People should not concern themselves with things that are not their business.

   Ⓓ Helping others is rewarding.

4. **What lesson did the wise king teach his subjects?**

   Ⓐ More good comes from working hard than from complaining.

   Ⓑ A king is not responsible for his subjects.

   Ⓒ Everyone is equally important.

   Ⓓ Always expect a difficult task to be rewarding.

Write It Right

Rewrite each sentence and correct the errors.

1. did you ride on won of the paddle boats along the missouri river

_____

_____

2. larry shouted to one of his friend's at the game look at that

_____

_____

3. snails grasshoppers and other bugs nibbled on the plants in aunt mays garden

_____

_____

MATH TIME

Use the rule listed at the top of each function table to help you complete the tables.
The first ones have been done for you.

Rule: ×2 +3	
Input	Output
1	5
2	
7	
	13
	19
	37

Rule: ×9 ÷3	
Input	Output
1	3
	15
8	
	21
12	
	45

SPELL IT

There are several ways to spell words with the /ər/ sound:

ir   er   ar   ear   or   ur

Fill in the letters that stand for the /ər/ sound in the spelling words for the week.

1. p _____ pose

2. _____ gent

3. th _____ sty

4. c _____ tain

5. wond _____

6. gramm _____

7. calend _____

8. _____ th

9. _____ ly

10. may _____

11. smuggl _____

12. p _____ l

In My Own Words

What if you woke up one day on another planet? Write the beginning of a story, telling how you felt, what you saw, and the first thing you did.

LANGUAGE LINES

Underline the pronoun in the second sentence of each pair. On the line, write the noun that the pronoun replaced.

1. The bus is coming. It is late.   _____

2. Mr. Jefferson is the driver. He is usually on time.   _____

3. Isaiah and Felicia are laughing. They love a joke.   _____

4. Carmen is laughing. She is usually reading quietly.   _____

5. Tony sits next to Carlos. Tony is grinning at him.   _____

6. Carlos is looking at Rosa. Carlos is smiling at her.   _____

7. Why are the kids laughing? What happened to them?   _____

8. My brother Ian and I want to know. What did we miss?   _____

9. Tony looks at Ian and me. Then Tony tells us.   _____

10. Tony, Ian, and I laugh. We laugh the whole way to school.   _____

MATH TIME

Solve the word problems about a camping trip taken by a group of Scouts.

1. During the camping trip, 9 Scouts can sleep in a cabin. All boys or all girls must sleep in each cabin. If there are 70 boys and 76 girls, how many cabins will be needed to house all of the Scouts?

2. The camping trip costs $25.00 per Scout. If there are 146 Scouts going on the trip, how much money will the Scouts need in all?

3. The Scouts held a fundraiser to help pay for the trip. They raised $1,562. If they split the money between all 146 Scouts, how much will each Scout still owe for the trip? Round to the nearest dollar.

Answer: _____

Answer: _____

Answer: _____

Read the article. Then answer the questions.

Libraries to Go

In the small villages of Kenya, Africa, most kids want to read books. But no roads lead to their homes, just miles and miles of sand. Cars and trucks are useless. So library books arrive on the backs of camels. Camels can handle the sand *and* the books. Two camels, a camel driver, and a librarian walk to the villages. One camel carries about 400 pounds of books, and the other carries a tent. At each village, the librarian sets up the tent and displays the books inside. Two weeks later, the camels return with new books.

Some people who live in the mountains and jungles of northern Thailand rely on a different kind of animal to bring their books. Their "libraries" are carried on the backs of elephants. These massive mammals can handle the difficult journey. Because of their size, they can carry heavy loads of books in metal cases. The metal protects the books from the heavy rains that fall in the area.

The country of Indonesia has a different challenge. This country is made up of over 17,000 islands. Therefore, most people travel by boat, and so do their library books. A wooden library boat holds about 500 books packed in boxes. Boxes of books are left in villages and are traded for new books a few weeks later.

For people who live in a remote area and can't get to a library, a library that comes to *them* brings more than books. It brings a whole world of information.

· ·

1. **Why do camels deliver library books to some villages in Kenya?**

   Ⓐ They can handle all of the rain.

   Ⓑ They can walk in the sand and carry heavy loads.

   Ⓒ They can carry the books in metal cases.

   Ⓓ They can travel through the jungles.

2. **Boats carry library books in Indonesia because _____.**

   Ⓐ boats are faster than elephants

   Ⓑ the villages are surrounded by sand

   Ⓒ the jungles are too hard to walk through

   Ⓓ people live on many different islands

3. **Because of the heavy rain in Thailand, _____.**

   Ⓐ camels carry library books

   Ⓑ library books are placed in metal cases

   Ⓒ boats deliver library books

   Ⓓ elephants carry tents and library books

4. **Based on the passage, which conclusion can be made?**

   Ⓐ Reading is important to people around the world.

   Ⓑ All libraries are buildings.

   Ⓒ Camels and elephants are intelligent.

   Ⓓ Boats work better than any other method for delivering books.

Vo•cab•u•lar•y

Homophones are words that sound alike but have different spellings and different meanings.

Complete each set of sentences with a pair or group of homophones from the box.

their, there, they're	pail, pale	your, you're	who's, whose
stationary, stationery	pray, prey	side, sighed	

1. "Everyone is against me. No one is on my _____," said Pablo.

   Then he _____ deeply and sunk down on the couch.

2. I went to the _____ store to buy a get-well card for my uncle, who

   broke his leg. He must stay completely _____ for at least a week.

3. Who's that over _____? Do you think it's the Silverman sisters and

   _____ parents? Maybe _____ walking home.

4. If _____ going to the park this afternoon, will you please take

   _____ little brother?

5. My dog thinks that he is a predator and squirrels are his _____.

   For the squirrels' sake, I _____ that my dog never catches one.

6. I watched my little sister play on the beach in the _____ morning

   light. She used a _____ and shovel to build a sand castle.

7. Do you know _____ responsible for this mess? If you know

   _____ toys are scattered all over the living room, please tell me.

LANGUAGE LINES

A **verb** must agree in number with its subject. If the subject is singular, the verb must be singular. If the subject is plural, the verb must be plural.

Read each sentence. If the subject-verb agreement is correct, write *correct* on the line. If the subject-verb agreement is *not* correct, rewrite the sentence correctly.

1. At the Aquarium, I learns about coral reefs.

   _____

2. Our guide teaches us about jellyfish.

   _____

3. Carla and Joe likes the shark tank.

   _____

4. We ask the guide a lot of questions.

   _____

In My Own Words

Imagine you found a $100 bill lying on the ground. What would you do with the money?

© Evan-Moor Corp. • EMC 1066 • Daily Summer Activities

Mind Jigglers

Who Ate What?

The Jones family went out for dinner. Each person ordered something different. Read the clues and fill in the chart to find out what each person ordered. Make an **X** in a box when it *cannot* be an answer. Draw a circle in the box when it is the correct answer.

	Grandpa	Grandma	Dad	Mom	Josh	Becca
Hamburger						
Lasagna						
Fish and chips						
Baked salmon						
Spaghetti						
Chicken strips						

1. None of the males in the family ordered a dinner that contained pasta.

2. None of the adults ordered a hamburger.

3. The person who ordered spaghetti is younger than the person who ordered lasagna.

4. Dad is allergic to fish.

5. Grandma did not order lasagna.

6. The person who ordered salmon shared some of it with his wife.

© Evan-Moor Corp. • EMC 1066 • Daily Summer Activities

MATH TIME

Find the Volume

Jamal wants to buy the fish tank that will hold the most water. Determine the volume of each rectangular prism. Circle the tank with the greatest volume.

 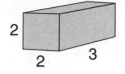

1. _____

2. _____

3. _____

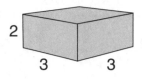 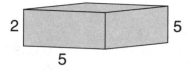

4. _____

5. _____

6. _____

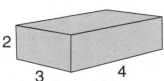 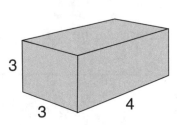 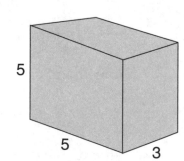

7. _____

8. _____

9. _____

Geography

Montana Road Map

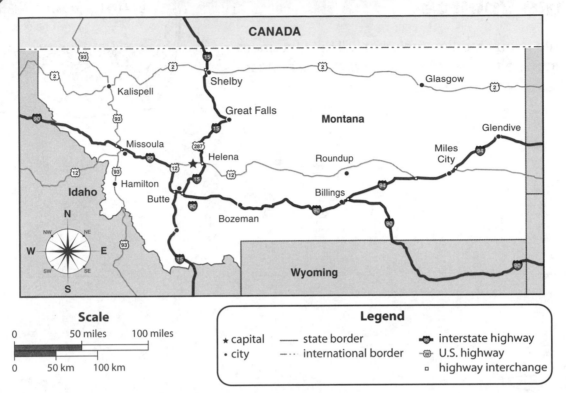

Scale

0   50 miles   100 miles

0   50 km   100 km

Legend

★ capital   —— state border   interstate highway
• city   -·-·- international border   U.S. highway
                                             ▫ highway interchange

Use the map to answer the questions.

1. There are two major kinds of roads on this map. What are they called?

_____

2. Name the two highways that run in a north-south direction through Montana.

_____

3. Name all of the labeled cities on or right next to Interstate 90.

_____

4. Estimate the distance from Billings to Glendive.

_____

WEEK 5

Check off each box as you complete the day's work.

Spelling Words

answer

design

doubt

honor

island

knapsack

knowledge

limb

listen

talking

whistle

wrestle

Get Creative!

Draw your favorite food.

A Memorable Moment

What sticks in your mind about this week? Write about it.

_____

_____

_____

_____

_____

_____

Reading Record

	Book Title	Pages	Time
Monday	_____	_____	_____
Tuesday	_____	_____	_____
Wednesday	_____	_____	_____
Thursday	_____	_____	_____
Friday	_____	_____	_____

Describe a character you read about this week.

_____

_____

_____

_____

_____

Read the story. Then answer the questions.

A Perfect Job?

Ben and Oscar decided that pet-sitting would be the perfect summer job. So Ben designed a flier, and the boys posted it at the pet store, Petrie's Pet Palace.

A few days later, the boys got their first job. A man named Chuck asked them to feed his lizard. Oscar hoped the lizard would be a giant Gila monster with claws as sharp as razors. Ben imagined the lizard as a Komodo dragon with long shark-like teeth. But when the boys went to Chuck's house that afternoon to get instructions, they were surprised to see a puny green reptile in a tank full of leaves. Chuck said the lizard's name was Gizzard.

The next day, Ben overslept, so the boys had to rush to Chuck's house. Ben checked on Gizzard while Oscar went to get the crickets to feed him. As Oscar reached for the bag in the fridge, he heard Ben yell, "Oscar, get over here! You won't believe what happened to Gizzard! He's already starved to death! All that's left of him is his shriveled skin!"

The boys ran to the pet shop and bought a replacement. When they returned to Chuck's house, Ben started to put the new lizard in the tank. Then he exclaimed with surprise, "Hey, there's Gizzard! And there's his skin! He didn't die—he just molted."

"You should have looked in the tank more closely," Oscar said, frowning. "Now our first pet-sitting job cost *us* $20."

. . . .

1. **Whom is the story about?**
   - Ⓐ a man who owns a pet shop
   - Ⓑ a man who has a lizard
   - Ⓒ a lizard that dies and comes back to life
   - Ⓓ two boys pet-sitting a lizard

2. **Which adjective best describes Ben?**
   - Ⓐ adventuresome
   - Ⓑ careless
   - Ⓒ successful
   - Ⓓ embarrassed

3. **Where does most of the story take place?**
   - Ⓐ at Chuck's house and at school
   - Ⓑ at the pet store and Oscar's house
   - Ⓒ at Chuck's house and the pet store
   - Ⓓ at Oscar's house and Chuck's house

4. **What length of time does the story cover?**
   - Ⓐ the entire summer
   - Ⓑ a few days
   - Ⓒ the last three days of school
   - Ⓓ one afternoon

Write It Right

Rewrite each sentence and correct the errors.

1. can you come with my friends and i to central park

_____

2. is adam spending august at lake mead or is he staying home

_____

3. tammi shouted keep away from that broken bottle

_____

4. me and tracie is going to the mall on saterday

_____

MATH TIME

Complete the addition problems.

2.5	1.2	4.29	92.5	91.64
+ 6.4	+ 6.7	+ 4.31	+ 43.8	+ 15.28

24.90	15.300	12.5	51.6	21.951
+ 6.52	+ 5.915	+ 2.9	+ 4.0	+ 5.319

15.3	49.2	15.0	4.23	4.29
+ 84.6	+ 6.5	+ 6.4	+ 6.51	+ 93.34

© Evan-Moor Corp. • EMC 1066 • Daily Summer Activities

SPELL IT

Many words have consonants that are **silent**. For example, the **t** is silent in the words **castle** and **hustle**.

Fill in the letters to complete the spelling words for the week. Then circle the silent consonant or consonants in each word.

1. w ____ es ____ ____ e

2. an ____ ____ er

3. dou ____ ____

4. ____ ____ apsack

5. li ____ ____ en

6. ____ ____ land

7. ta ____ ____ ing

8. desi ____ ____

9. k ____ ____ wle ____ ____ e

10. li ____ ____

11. ____ ____ nor

12. whi ____ ____ ____ e

In My Own Words

If you could have a superpower, which one would you choose? How would you use your new power?

LANGUAGE LINES

An adjective describes a noun or a pronoun.

Underline the adjectives in the sentences.

1. Imagine going to a big cinema to see a silent movie.

2. You find a comfortable seat and watch the large, dark screen light up.

3. You expect the movie to be exciting and entertaining.

4. It stars a handsome actor and a beautiful actress, both of whom are famous celebrities.

5. But when they appear on the huge screen, you do not hear their voices.

6. Silent movies displayed words on the screen to tell stories that could be funny or serious.

7. The actors also exaggerated their facial expressions to show dramatic emotions.

8. You had to be a good, fast reader to watch a silent film.

9. Today, movies not only have sound but amazing effects.

10. These effects can make going to a movie a memorable—and loud—experience!

MATH TIME

Complete the subtraction problems.

61.2 − 60.1	5.9 − 2.3	4.1 − 3.9	12.9 − 9.2	15.9 − 7.8
12.1 − 5.8	15.26 − 5.49	4.59 − 2.00	83.49 − 2.95	8.00 − 5.12
51.2 − 14.1	96.0 − 5.8	49.2 − 15.9	91.0 − 2.5	16.29 − 5.49

Read the article. Then answer the questions.

Where the Wild Things Are

Baloo lies on his back, huge and furry. Shere Khan nuzzles his face and rubs his whiskers into Baloo's neck. Leo stretches in the grass near a rock and yawns with a slight roar. The three animals live together in a fenced-in space, and they share a small wooden house. But they are not pets. They are fully grown wild animals. Baloo the bear, Leo the lion, and Shere Khan the tiger were each rescued in 2001 when they were two-month-old cubs. They were taken to Noah's Ark Animal Center in Georgia, and they have never been separated since then. Their young age helped them form an unusual friendship.

Baloo and Shere Khan were named after characters in *The Jungle Book*. They play together during the day while Leo sleeps. When Leo wakes up, the three friends wrestle and play like brothers before Baloo and Shere Khan go to sleep. Sometimes they pile on top of each other for warmth and to show affection.

In the wild, these three would live in different habitats. Black bears usually live in forested areas. African grasslands are home to lions, while tigers survive in the jungles of Asia. But Baloo, Shere Khan, and Leo don't know what it's like to live in the wild. None of these animals hunt for their own food. Instead, they are fed by the humans who care for them. None of the animals know how unusual—or special—their friendship is.

· ·

1. **How are the three animals alike?**

   Ⓐ In the wild, they would all live in forests.

   Ⓑ They are all named for characters in a book.

   Ⓒ They were all rescued at the same time.

   Ⓓ They are all active during the day.

2. **Unlike Baloo and Shere Khan, Leo is _____.**

   Ⓐ wild

   Ⓑ a meat eater

   Ⓒ more active at night

   Ⓓ a vegetarian

3. **Based on the passage, which one of these is true?**

   Ⓐ Different animals cannot live together.

   Ⓑ Bears prefer lions to tigers.

   Ⓒ Zoos are the best place for any animal.

   Ⓓ Bears usually have a different home than lions do.

4. **Which one is true about Baloo?**

   Ⓐ He is fed by people who care for him.

   Ⓑ He is most active at night.

   Ⓒ He prefers Shere Khan to Leo.

   Ⓓ He prefers to sleep by himself.

Vo·cab·u·lar·y

A **compound word** is a word made up of two or more smaller words. You might see the same smaller word in many different compound words.

Write the compound word that best replaces the underlined words in each sentence. Use a dictionary to help you, if necessary.

uphold	upbeat	update	uproar
upstream	backdrop	backtracked	backfired

1. The news of the soccer team's victory put our school in a major <u>state of noisy confusion</u>. _____

2. Pablo's scheme to trick his friend <u>ended up causing the opposite effect from the one he wanted</u>. His friend tricked him, instead! _____

3. The play's first act took place in front of a forest <u>scene painted at the back of the stage</u>. _____

4. Andrea writes mournful poems, but my poems are more <u>cheerful and optimistic</u>. _____

5. One of the government's jobs is to <u>protect and defend</u> people's civil rights. _____

6. Arguing in favor of an unpopular plan can be like swimming <u>against the current</u>. _____

7. Mom asked for an <u>explanation of the latest details</u> on my math grade. _____

8. When I noticed that I'd lost a mitten, I <u>retraced my steps</u> until I found it. _____

© Evan-Moor Corp. • EMC 1066 • Daily Summer Activities

LANGUAGE LINES

Write the correct negative from the word box to complete each sentence.

> no   not   never   nowhere

1. Shirenda _____ remembers her sister's birthday.

2. She has _____ idea why it's so hard to remember.

3. We _____ forget Shauna's birthday.

4. We know that Shauna will go _____ on her birthday without Shirenda.

5. There is _____ way we're going to let Shirenda forget again.

6. This year, Shirenda does _____ stand a chance!

7. We'll _____ let her rest until she has bought a card and a present.

8. This is _____ going to be like any other year for Shauna.

In My Own Words

Have you ever had something weird or scary happen to you? Describe the event.

Mind Jigglers

Playful Plates

Some people have special license plates with letters and numbers that create a message. What do the plates below say? The first one has been done for you.

IML8

1. ___I'm late.___

LUV2SKI

2. _____

RUHAPE

3. _____

CR8TIV

4. _____

ICU2

5. _____

L8R G8R

6. _____

1GR8GAL

7. _____

CRAZ4U

8. _____

QT PIE

9. _____

UR2SLO

10. _____

© Evan-Moor Corp. • EMC 1066 • Daily Summer Activities

MATH TIME

The Solar System

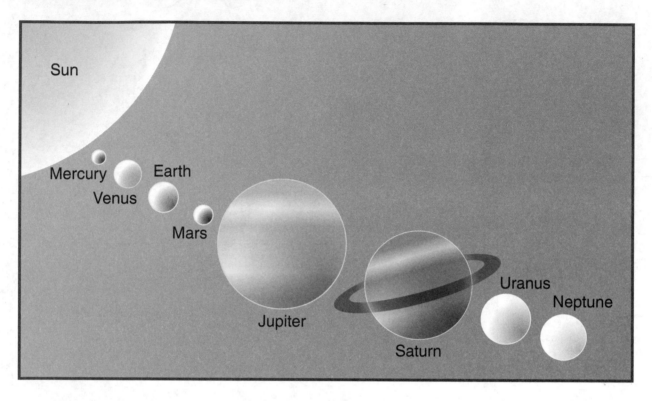

1. Mercury is about 58 million kilometers from the sun, and Earth is about 155 million kilometers from the sun. How much farther away from the sun is Earth than Mercury?

   _____

2. The diameter of Earth is 12,756 kilometers, the diameter of Saturn is 120,600 kilometers, and the diameter of Uranus is 51,300 kilometers. Is the sum of these three planets more or less than Jupiter's diameter of 142,200 kilometers? How much more or less is it?

   _____

3. A year on Jupiter is about 12 Earth years. If a year on Earth is 365 days, how many days would a year be on Jupiter?

   _____

Geography

Product Map of Nebraska

Major Farm Products

- beef cattle
- hogs
- corn
- soybeans

Nebraska

This product map shows the natural products that are grown or raised in Nebraska. Use the map to answer the questions.

1. In which part of Nebraska are most of the farm products grown or raised—in the northwest, southwest, southeast, or northeast? _____

2. Is Nebraska located in the northeastern, western, north-central, or southern region of the United States? _____

3. What are the major crops grown in Nebraska?

   _____

4. Which types of livestock are shown on the map?

   _____

West of Greenwich   Longitude West of Greenwich

120°   B   150°   C   180°   D   150°   E   120°   F   90°

WEEK 6

Check off each box as you complete the day's work.

Spelling Words

briefly

enough

fountain

fourth

fragile

graph

nephew

pharmacy

physical

roughest

staff

triumph

Get Creative!

If you ruled your own country, what would your flag look like? Draw it!

A Memorable Moment

What sticks in your mind about this week? Write about it.

_____

_____

_____

_____

_____

_____

Reading Record

	Book Title	Pages	Time
Monday	_____	_____	_____
Tuesday	_____	_____	_____
Wednesday	_____	_____	_____
Thursday	_____	_____	_____
Friday	_____	_____	_____

Describe a character you read about this week.

_____

_____

_____

_____

_____

Read the article. Then answer the questions.

Life on Jupiter's Icy Moon

Jupiter is the largest planet in our solar system and is made up of many different kinds of gases. It is so big that 1,300 Earths could fit *inside* Jupiter! It also has 63 moons. Some of its moons are like small planets, and others are pieces of frozen rock and ice. Studying Jupiter's moons has helped scientists learn more about the solar system. But the moon that scientists are most interested in is Europa (yur-OH-pa).

The conditions on Europa make it the most likely place in the solar system, besides Earth, to have life. It is covered in a layer of ice, and some scientists believe a liquid ocean lies beneath the icy surface. If this is true, Europa may have simple forms of life in these oceans. The creatures on Europa would probably be too small to see without a microscope. But the idea of anything at all living on Europa is very exciting.

Right now, we cannot explore Europa because it is too cold and too far away to send people there. The spacecrafts and robots we have are not sturdy enough to land on the surface. But scientists have big plans. In the future, they hope to send one robot to melt some of the ice on Europa's surface, and another robot to swim through its oceans. The information that these robots gather could change what we think about life beyond Earth.

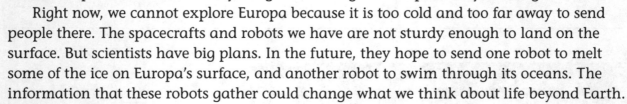

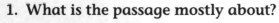

1. **What is the passage mostly about?**
   - Ⓐ Jupiter's many moons
   - Ⓑ possible life on Europa
   - Ⓒ scientists' search for new life
   - Ⓓ the problem with exploring outer space

2. **Which of these explains why scientists think life could exist on Europa?**
   - Ⓐ The creatures would be too small to see without a microscope.
   - Ⓑ Europa is one of Jupiter's 63 moons.
   - Ⓒ Europa has a layer of ice that may have liquid below it.
   - Ⓓ Jupiter is the solar system's largest planet.

3. **What is the main idea of the last paragraph?**
   - Ⓐ Exploring Europa is very difficult.
   - Ⓑ People are better than robots.
   - Ⓒ Scientists want to discover new life.
   - Ⓓ Life can only be discovered by machines.

4. **Europa is best described as _____.**
   - Ⓐ warm and full of life
   - Ⓑ cold and uninteresting
   - Ⓒ icy and mysterious
   - Ⓓ cool and dry

Write It Right

Rewrite each sentence and correct the errors.

1. that greedy little child drinked all the cold lemonade they done had

   _____

   _____

2. terrys brothers afraid of the dark so his mom gived him a flashlight

   _____

   _____

3. my mothers favorite poem by robert frost is the road not taken

   _____

   _____

MATH TIME

Complete the multiplication problems.

1. 2.0 x 0.1 = _____

2. 4.0 x 0.5 = _____

3. 8.0 x 0.25 = _____

4. 5.0 x 0.5 = _____

5. 1.0 x 0.75 = _____

6. 3.5 x 0.5 = _____

7. 3.0 x 0.25 = _____

8. 2.0 x 0.4 = _____

9. 5.0 x 0.8 = _____

10. 4.0 x 0.95 = _____

11. 2.0 x 0.87 = _____

12. 6.5 x 0.4 = _____

SPELL IT

The sound **/f/** can be spelled several ways:

f   ph   gh   ff

Fill in the blanks with the letter or letters that stand for the **/f/** sound to make the spelling words for the week.

1. gra _____

2. ne _____ ew

3. enou _____

4. _____ ourth

5. _____ ysical

6. rou _____ est

7. _____ armacy

8. _____ ragile

9. brie _____ ly

10. trium _____

11. _____ ountain

12. sta _____

In My Own Words

Name a character from a book that you can identify with.
Explain how you are similar to or different from that character.

LANGUAGE LINES

A **prepositional phrase** is made up of a preposition, the object of the preposition, and any words in between. Some prepositional phrases describe verbs and adverbs.

Underline the prepositional phrase in each sentence. Draw an arrow from the prepositional phrase to the verb or adverb it describes. Then circle *when* or *where* to explain what the phrase tells. The first one has been done for you.

1. The rain falls from the sky.   when   (where)
2. I hear the water rushing down the windows.   when   where
3. The lightning crackles before each thunderbolt.   when   where
4. I creep deeper under my quilt.   when   where
5. The house shakes after each jolt as the storm rages.   when   where
6. The wind screams loudly through the trees outside.   when   where
7. I worry that the roof might blow off the house.   when   where
8. I wonder if a tornado is headed toward us!   when   where

MATH TIME

Solve the word problems about earning money.

1. Max walked dogs to earn money. He charged $16 per week to walk one dog for 30 minutes per day. He walked 21 dogs every week. How much money did he earn in four weeks?

   Answer: _____

2. Arturo mowed lawns to earn money. He mowed 14 lawns each week and charged $24 to mow each one. How much did he earn in 12 weeks?

   Answer: _____

3. Cathy and Chris sold homemade cookies for $6 a bag. The girls sold 180 bags. Half of the money they collected paid for the cookie ingredients. The other half was their profit. How much profit did the girls make?

   Answer: _____

© Evan-Moor Corp. • EMC 1066 • Daily Summer Activities

Read the story. Then answer the questions.

The Boy Who Cried "Pirates!"

Long ago, a boy named Johnny lived on a ship that sailed the seas. His father was the captain. Johnny continually begged his father to let him keep watch.

"Life on the sea is dangerous," his father said. "Only the most responsible sailors can keep watch for sudden storms or fearsome pirates."

One night, after much complaining and begging, the captain allowed Johnny to keep watch. Johnny expected the work to be exciting, but time crept more slowly than a slug. So Johnny decided to have some fun.

"Pirates! Pirates!" Johnny yelled out. The sailors scrambled on deck, only to see Johnny laughing. "Just kidding!" he said as his eyes filled with tears of laughter.

The captain was furious. "Pirates are no joke," he scolded. He made Johnny promise to behave, but Johnny did not listen. Once again, when everyone was asleep, he sounded the alarm. Sleepy sailors hurried to their posts, ready for action. And again, Johnny laughed at the fun of tricking them.

The third time Johnny was on watch, he yawned and stretched, scanning the horizon. To his shock, he saw an actual pirate ship in the distance. "P-p-pirates!" he stammered. "PIRATES!" But the sailors merely rolled over in their hammocks. They were sure Johnny was lying again. As the pirate ship edged closer, Johnny's heart beat quickly with fear. He realized that there was nothing funny about this.

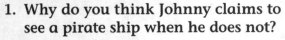

1. **Why do you think Johnny claims to see a pirate ship when he does not?**

   Ⓐ to disobey his father, the captain

   Ⓑ to prove he has better eyes than the sailors

   Ⓒ to trick the sailors

   Ⓓ to show that he is young but brave

2. **Why does Johnny continue to lie?**

   Ⓐ He likes fooling the others.

   Ⓑ The sailors do not seem to mind.

   Ⓒ He does not know he is lying.

   Ⓓ The captain tells him to lie.

3. **How does Johnny change at the end?**

   Ⓐ He was lazy but becomes hardworking.

   Ⓑ He was helpful but decides to be a pirate.

   Ⓒ He was foolish but realizes his mistakes.

   Ⓓ He was silly but becomes trustworthy.

4. **What is a theme of the story?**

   Ⓐ You should ask for help even if you do not need it.

   Ⓑ Standing watch on a ship is boring.

   Ⓒ You can trick people forever.

   Ⓓ Liars are not believed, even when they tell the truth.

Vo·cab·u·lar·y

Antonyms are words with opposite meanings. For example, **happy** is an antonym of **sad**.

A. Complete each sentence by writing an antonym from the box on the line above the word in parentheses.

villain	accept	public	certain
original	youthful	sensible	professional

1. Which is the most _____ solution to our problem?
    (foolish)

2. I've never seen the _____ of that famous painting.
    (copy)

3. The president's inauguration is a _____ ceremony.
    (private)

4. Uncle Dave plans to _____ the job offer.
    (refuse)

5. Our dog is 14 years old, but she still acts _____.
    (elderly)

6. Some _____ athletes earn millions of dollars a year.
    (amateur)

7. I studied for the test all weekend, so I'm _____ I will pass.
    (doubtful)

8. By the end of a fairy tale, the _____ is usually caught.
    (hero)

B. Choose a pair of antonyms from one of the sentences in Activity A. Write a sentence using both words.

_____

_____

© Evan-Moor Corp. • EMC 1066 • Daily Summer Activities

LANGUAGE LINES

Clipped words are shortened forms of longer words.

In each sentence, replace the underlined word with the correct clipped word from the box.

> vet   fan   tie   champ   flu   pop   mini   burger

1. George is a soccer <u>fanatic</u>.   _____

2. Rachel always listens to the station that plays <u>popular</u> music.   _____

3. My sister has a <u>miniature</u> refrigerator in her dorm room.   _____

4. Mom ordered a <u>hamburger</u> and fries.   _____

5. Dan is the state diving <u>champion</u>.   _____

6. Have you gotten your <u>influenza</u> shot yet?   _____

7. Dad hates having to wear a <u>necktie</u> every day to work.   _____

8. Max's grandfather is an army <u>veteran</u>.   _____

In My Own Words

Write a "how-to" paragraph explaining something you know how to make or do.

Map Grid of Australia

To read a map grid, first look at the letter rows and then look at the number columns. Each box on the grid helps you find a specific location.

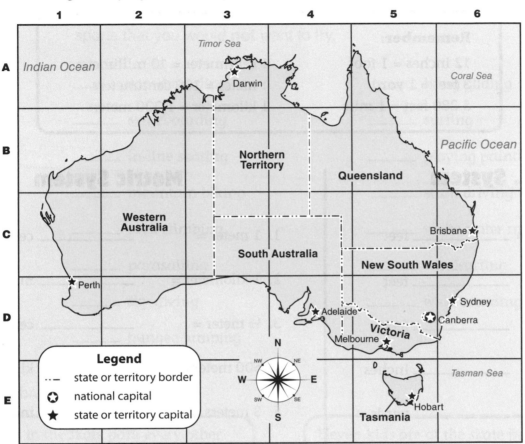

Use the map grid to answer the questions.

1. Which city is located at A3? _____

2. Which state is located at E5? _____

3. Brisbane is the capital of which state? _____

4. What is the capital of Western Australia? _____

5. Which state is in C3, C4, D3, and D4? _____

6. Which bodies of water surround Australia? _____

_____

WEEK 7

Check off the box as you complete the day's work.

Spelling Words

already

appreciate

attendance

business

cough

discipline

embarrass

occasion

rhythm

separate

sincerely

traveler

Get Creative!

Turn this line into a robot.

A Memorable Moment

What sticks in your mind about this week? Write about it.

_____

_____

_____

_____

_____

_____

Reading Record

Book Title	Pages	Time
Monday _____	_____	_____
Tuesday _____	_____	_____
Wednesday _____	_____	_____
Thursday _____	_____	_____
Friday _____	_____	_____

Describe a character you read about this week.

_____

_____

_____

_____

_____

_____

Read the article. Then answer the questions.

A Patient Parent

Adults may tell you that it's tough being a parent. But they have it easy compared to the emperor penguin. This parent has one of the toughest jobs in the animal kingdom.

Emperor penguins mate in Antarctica in March or April. The female lays an egg in May or June. Then the mother penguin carefully passes the egg to the father, who balances it on top of his feet. The penguins must be very careful not to drop the egg, as it can crack or freeze if it touches the ground.

The mother leaves to find food, and the father waits patiently for the egg to hatch. This usually takes at least 60 days. During that time, the father doesn't eat, and he must stay very still so he doesn't hurt the egg.

By the time the chick hatches, the father is very weak. But he must feed the baby if the mother has not yet returned. He does this by making a special liquid in his throat. Luckily the mother penguin usually returns within a few days after the chick hatches. She feeds the chick and takes care of it so the father can go get food for himself. By this time, the male has gone 115 days without eating. Talk about a devoted dad!

. . . .

1. **What does the mother penguin do right after she lays the egg?**

   Ⓐ She finds food.

   Ⓑ She gives the egg to the father.

   Ⓒ She takes care of the egg.

   Ⓓ She lets the father eat.

2. **What always happens before the chick hatches?**

   Ⓐ The father leaves to find food.

   Ⓑ The mother returns to care for the chick.

   Ⓒ The father doesn't eat and barely moves.

   Ⓓ The mother and father care for the chick together.

3. **Which of these does *not* happen after the chick hatches?**

   Ⓐ The mother feeds the chick.

   Ⓑ The mother returns with food.

   Ⓒ The father leaves to find food.

   Ⓓ The father sits without eating or moving.

4. **What is the last thing that happens after emperor penguins mate?**

   Ⓐ The chick hatches from its egg.

   Ⓑ The parents take turns caring for the chick.

   Ⓒ The father leaves to eat.

   Ⓓ The mother lays a new egg.

Write It Right

Rewrite each sentence and correct the errors.

1. my brother and me need to bye shirts pants socks and shoes for school

   _____

2. when will the technician ms rawlings fix ours computer

   _____

3. they all singed happy birthday before her cut the cake

   _____

4. we ain't got no fancy clothes for graduashun tomorow

   _____

MATH TIME

Solve the multiplication problems.

$\frac{3}{4}$ x $\frac{1}{2}$ = _____

$\frac{2}{5}$ x $\frac{1}{3}$ = _____

$\frac{4}{7}$ x $\frac{1}{3}$ = _____

$\frac{2}{5}$ x $\frac{4}{5}$ = _____

$\frac{1}{2}$ x $\frac{1}{6}$ = _____

$\frac{3}{4}$ x $\frac{1}{5}$ = _____

$\frac{5}{6}$ x $\frac{5}{7}$ = _____

$\frac{1}{5}$ x $\frac{2}{3}$ = _____

$\frac{4}{7}$ x $\frac{1}{9}$ = _____

$\frac{5}{9}$ x $\frac{4}{7}$ = _____

$\frac{1}{3}$ x $\frac{2}{7}$ = _____

$\frac{7}{8}$ x $\frac{3}{5}$ = _____

$\frac{1}{8}$ x $\frac{3}{8}$ = _____

$\frac{5}{8}$ x $\frac{3}{7}$ = _____

$\frac{1}{2}$ x $\frac{5}{9}$ = _____

$\frac{2}{5}$ x $\frac{3}{7}$ = _____

$\frac{7}{9}$ x $\frac{10}{11}$ = _____

$\frac{1}{3}$ x $\frac{10}{13}$ = _____

SPELL IT

Words that are often misspelled are called **spelling demons**.

Circle the correct spelling of each spelling demon.

1. separate   seperate
2. travelor   traveler
3. embarass   embarrass
4. occasion   ocassion
5. allready   already
6. coff   cough

7. busness   business
8. attendance   attendence
9. discipline   disipline
10. rhythym   rhythm
11. appreciate   apreciate
12. sincerly   sincerely

In My Own Words

In the story *Alice in Wonderland*, Alice fell down a rabbit hole and had many adventures. Imagine that you fell down a hole into a different world. Describe an adventure you might have.

LANGUAGE LINES

A **sentence** must express a complete thought. A group of words
that does not express a complete thought is called a **fragment**.

Write *sentence* if the group of words expresses a complete thought and *fragment* if it does not.

1. The volcanoes of New Zealand. _____

2. Volcanoes formed New Zealand. _____

3. The ash and lava created interesting landforms. _____

4. With active volcanoes nearby. _____

5. New Zealanders live near active volcanoes. _____

6. Live on ranches in New Zealand. _____

7. Millions of sheep live on ranches. _____

8. Rugby, a kind of football. _____

9. New Zealanders love to play rugby. _____

MATH TIME

Solve the word problems.

1. Danny has 48 baseball cards in his collection. He would like to give $\frac{3}{4}$ of them to his little brother. How many should he give his brother?

   Answer: _____

2. Mary Anne has 60 troll dolls in her bedroom. Her parents have asked her to put $\frac{2}{3}$ of them away in storage because her room is too messy. How many does she need to put into storage?

   Answer: _____

3. Miguel is collecting stamps. He has 120 pages in his stamp book. If $\frac{3}{5}$ of the pages are filled with stamps, how many blank pages are there in Miguel's book?

   Answer: _____

4. Brendan has a rock collection that weighs 200 pounds. His dad tried to lift it and realized it was too heavy. He was only able to lift $\frac{5}{8}$ of the collection at once. How many pounds of rocks was Brendan's dad able to lift?

   Answer: _____

Moor Corp. • EMC 1066 • Daily Summer Activities

Read the story. Then answer the questions.

Mighty Stormalong

Have you heard of Stormalong, the tallest, biggest sailor there ever was? When Stormalong was born, he was so big that he was given a tree branch for a rattle. When Stormalong was one year old, his mom and dad took the roof off the house so he wouldn't hit his head on it. Stormalong was taller than most buildings by the time he was two.

Stormalong's mom spent four years knitting a hammock for him to sleep in. It stretched from New Jersey to New York. Stormalong watched the ships sail up and down the Hudson River as he swayed in his bed.

When Stormalong turned 10 years old, he joined the crew of the *Humongous*. It was the biggest ship he could find. All went well as long as he stayed in the middle of the ship. But if he leaned to the side just a bit, the ship would lean, too, and the crew would tumble out.

Stormalong outgrew the *Humongous* when he was 13. So he built his own ship, the *Gigantic*. It was as fast as it was large. Stormalong decided to sail around the world. He left New York on a sunny day after a large breakfast of sausages as big as canoes. By the time he reached Florida, Stormalong was fast asleep. The *Gigantic* drifted south to Panama, the country that connects North America to South America. That ship was so big and heavy that it pushed right through the land and made the Panama Canal! Stormalong had created a shortcut between North and South America.

1. **Why did the author write the story?**

   Ⓐ to tell the life story of a famous sailor

   Ⓑ to persuade readers to write tales

   Ⓒ to explain how a canal was actually built

   Ⓓ to entertain readers with a silly tale about a giant

2. **Most of the author's descriptions of Stormalong are _____.**

   Ⓐ exaggerations

   Ⓑ historical facts

   Ⓒ comparisons

   Ⓓ opinions

3. **This story would most likely be found in a book _____.**

   Ⓐ about the history of the Panama Canal

   Ⓑ about famous sailing ships

   Ⓒ of stories about imaginary people

   Ⓓ about famous Americans

4. **The purpose of the last paragraph is to _____.**

   Ⓐ tell a made-up version of how a famous landmark was formed

   Ⓑ persuade people not to travel by ship

   Ⓒ make tall people feel proud

   Ⓓ describe an important sailing trip

Vo·cab·u·lar·y

Homographs are words that sound the same and are spelled the same but have different meanings. For example, the word **hatch** is a homograph. It can mean "a small opening with a door" or "to come out."

Raise the hatch to climb into the attic.   **Snakes hatch from eggs.**

Next to each sentence, write the letter that gives the meaning of the underlined homograph.

_____ 1. Put your dirty jeans in the <u>hamper</u>.

_____ 2. All of this rain will <u>hamper</u> the builders' progress.

_____ 3. Horses like to <u>graze</u> in the meadow.

_____ 4. Be careful not to <u>graze</u> your arm against the rough wooden fence.

_____ 5. Does your dog <u>bay</u> at the full moon?

_____ 6. There's a house on the cliff overlooking the <u>bay</u>.

_____ 7. The newborn lamb lies asleep in the <u>stall</u>.

_____ 8. This rainy weather might <u>stall</u> our plans to go fishing.

_____ 9. It is <u>rare</u> for me to have a soft drink.

_____ 10. The meat was too <u>rare</u>, so I cooked it longer.

_____ 11. I try to <u>refrain</u> from eating a lot of sugar.

_____ 12. The <u>refrain</u> is my favorite part of the song.

_____ 13. Be sure to lock the <u>stable</u> door.

_____ 14. I will keep the ladder <u>stable</u> as you climb.

a. firm, not shaky

b. to scrape

c. unusual; not often

d. a body of water near the coast

e. a basket for holding clothes

f. the chorus

g. cooked only for a short time

h. to hold oneself back from doing something

i. a pen inside a barn or stable

j. to disrupt or impede

k. to feed on growing grass

l. a building where animals are kept

m. to delay or prevent

n. to let out a long, howling bark

LANGUAGE LINES

The **subject** tells who or what the sentence is about.
The **predicate** tells what the subject is or does.

Write the complete subject and predicate of each sentence. The first one has been done for you.

1. The excited shoppers rush into the department store.

   The excited shoppers
   _____
   Subject

   rush into the department store
   _____
   Predicate

2. This denim jacket is on sale!

   _____
   Subject

   _____
   Predicate

3. We will eat lunch in a restaurant.

   _____
   Subject

   _____
   Predicate

4. This juicy hamburger with pickles tastes good.

   _____
   Subject

   _____
   Predicate

In My Own Words

Make a list of your five favorite foods. Explain why you like each one.

Mind Jigglers

Look at each grid with a shaded design. Then imagine how the design would look if the grid was turned 90 degrees to the right. Shade the squares in the second grid to show how the design would look. The first one has been done for you.

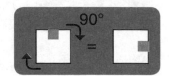

1.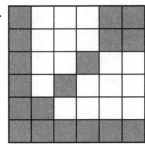

2.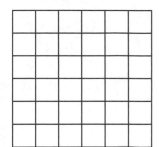

3.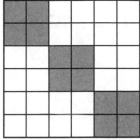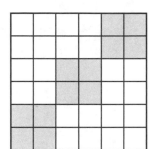

4.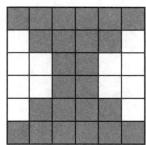

5.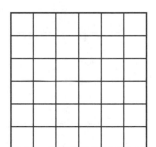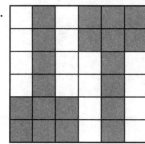

6.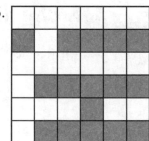

7.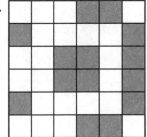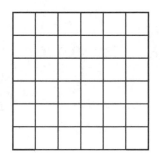

8.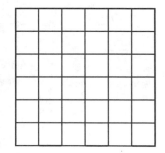

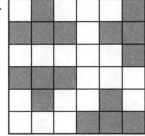 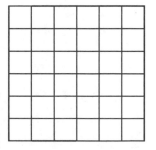 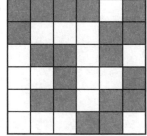 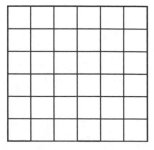

MATH TIME

Sports Stats

This table represents the different sports that boys and girls played at sports camp. Use the table to complete the double bar graph below for each sport.

	Football	Basketball	Soccer	Baseball	Golf
Boys	8	12	5	10	2
Girls	6	9	11	7	5

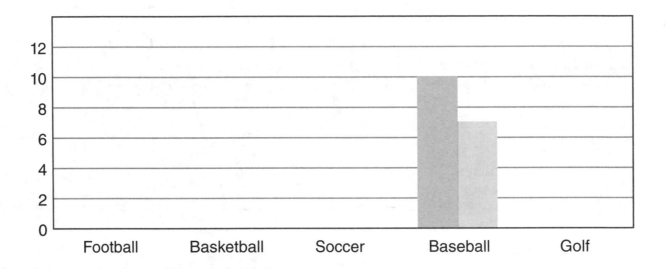

Use the table and graph to help you answer these questions.

1. How many more boys played basketball than girls? _____

2. Which sport did the most campers play? _____

3. Which sport did the fewest campers play? _____

4. Which sport did the girls play most? _____

5. Did more boys or girls attend sports camp? How many more? _____

Yellowstone National Park

1. How many entrances are there into Yellowstone National Park?

_____

2. Which entrance is the closest to the geyser called Old Faithful?

_____

3. Which is the largest lake in the park?

_____

4. Which point of interest is closest to the North Entrance?

_____

_____

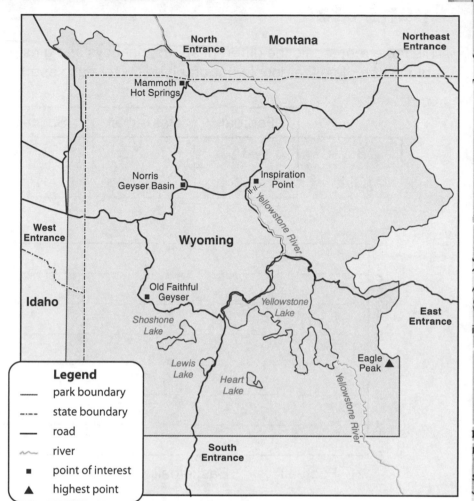

5. Inspiration Point is closest to which two labeled features?

_____

6. What is the highest point in Yellowstone National Park?

_____

7. Which lake is farthest west?

_____

WEEK 8

Check off each box as you complete the day's work.

Spelling Words

allow

committee

exaggerate

foreign

mischief

necessary

principle

receive

relieve

succeed

thorough

trouble

Get Creative!

Draw a picture to go with this caption: "Oh my, what a beautiful sunset."

A Memorable Moment

What sticks in your mind about this week? Write about it.

_____

_____

_____

_____

_____

_____

Reading Record

	Book Title	Pages	Time
Monday	_____	_____	_____
Tuesday	_____	_____	_____
Wednesday	_____	_____	_____
Thursday	_____	_____	_____
Friday	_____	_____	_____

Describe a character you read about this week.

_____

_____

_____

_____

_____

94

Read the story. Then answer the questions.

The Hungry Wolf and the Clever Fox

One moonlit night, Wolf was lurking in the forest, hoping to find dinner. He hadn't eaten all day, so he was grumpy from hunger. But his mood changed when he spied Fox trotting toward her den. Wolf boldly blocked Fox's path and spoke to her in a sweet voice.

"Fox, you certainly look beautiful tonight," Wolf said. "Your fur is so glossy."

When Fox saw Wolf's tongue droop and his mouth drool, she knew she had to think fast. Fox pointed to her fur and said, "Why, this old coat is full of ticks and fleas. I'm embarrassed to be seen in it." Fox tried to step away, but Wolf growled deeply.

"Don't move!" he snarled. "I'm hungry, and you look good enough to eat!"

"Mr. Wolf, I'm a skinny old thing," Fox said, jutting out her chin. "You'd be hungry again before you finished swallowing me. But I can show you where to get some delicious cheese. I know where there's a rich, creamy wheel of it as big as your head."

Even though his stomach growled terribly, Wolf was tempted by Fox's description of this magnificent cheese. He walked by her side until they came to a well. Wolf looked down and saw a large, round, yellow cheese floating in the water. As he leaned farther down into the well to gobble up the cheese, he lost his balance and tumbled into the well.

Fox chuckled. With the help of a full moon, she had outfoxed the Wolf.

· ·

1. **What was the result of Fox's trick?**

   Ⓐ She became friends with Wolf.

   Ⓑ She saved herself from being eaten.

   Ⓒ She was able to escape into a well.

   Ⓓ She had cheese to eat.

2. **What caused Wolf to stop and talk to Fox?**

   Ⓐ Fox was blocking his path home.

   Ⓑ Fox and Wolf were old friends.

   Ⓒ Wolf was hungry.

   Ⓓ Wolf was looking for some cheese.

3. **What caused Fox to try to trick Wolf?**

   Ⓐ She could tell that Wolf was hungry.

   Ⓑ She liked what Wolf said about her fur.

   Ⓒ She could hear Wolf's stomach growl.

   Ⓓ She was embarrassed by her coat.

4. **Why was Fox able to trick Wolf?**

   Ⓐ Fox was too skinny to be eaten.

   Ⓑ Wolf was angry with Fox.

   Ⓒ Fox was scared of Wolf.

   Ⓓ Wolf was distracted by his hunger.

Write It Right

Rewrite each sentence and correct the errors.

1. i cant never decide which i like best, halloween christmas or valentines day

_____

_____

2. after the bean seed sprouted it growed three inches in a week

_____

_____

3. get them dirty dogs of my clean sofa nana shouted with fustration

_____

_____

MATH TIME

Complete the division problems. Note the remainder when appropriate.

$24\overline{)491}$ $43\overline{)619}$ $25\overline{)6,429}$

$15\overline{)267}$ $19\overline{)826}$ $82\overline{)4,290}$

$43\overline{)915}$ $21\overline{)726}$ $37\overline{)3,000}$

SPELL IT

Fill in the missing syllables to complete the spelling words for the week.

1. trou _____

2. _____ ceed

3. al _____

4. _____ lieve

5. prin _____ ple

6. ex _____ gerate

7. mis _____

8. _____ eign

9. re _____

10. thor _____

11. _____ mittee

12. neces _____ y

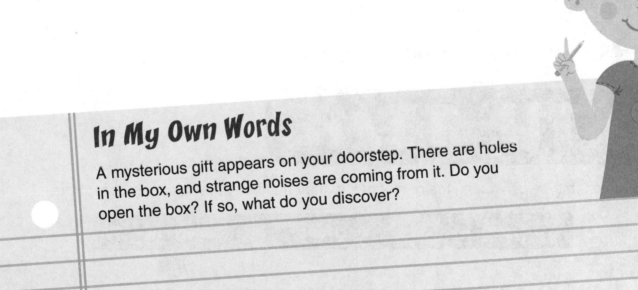

In My Own Words

A mysterious gift appears on your doorstep. There are holes in the box, and strange noises are coming from it. Do you open the box? If so, what do you discover?

LANGUAGE LINES

Verbs that are in the **past tense** show that an action has already taken place.

Above each verb in parentheses, write the past tense form of the verb. Watch out for spelling changes and irregular verb forms.

1. Our bus (stop) at the Ash Meadows National Wildlife Refuge.

2. Chris (study) the list of endangered animals in the guidebook.

3. He (read) us the story of the endangered Warm Springs pupfish.

4. Many kinds of birds (fly) in the sky overhead.

5. We (hurry) to see a bald eagle perched on a fence post.

6. Off in the distance, we (see) desert bighorn sheep.

7. The ranger (teach) us about the plants growing in the meadow.

MATH TIME

Complete the table by converting the numbers into their fraction, decimal, or percent forms.

Fraction	Decimal	Percent
		75%
	0.25	
$\frac{1}{2}$		
		30%
	0.6	
$\frac{1}{10}$		
	0.8	

Read the article. Then answer the questions.

Angry Animals

When the sun sets in Tasmania, a large island near Australia, spine-chilling screams pierce the air. The Tasmanian devils are awake and eager to eat. Tasmanian devils are mammals with ferocious appetites and tempers. If there is some meat to eat, dead or alive, these animals will go after it.

Tasmanian devils hunt alone, eating up to eight pounds of food a night. They gulp it down as fast as they can, and they don't share. They are scavengers that usually feed on dead animals such as birds or mammals. Their powerful jaws and sharp teeth can crush the toughest dinner. Every part of their meal gets eaten, including fur, feathers, and bones. Poisons and bacteria in the rotten meat do not harm the devils. They are like nature's garbage disposals. So even though they may seem disgusting, Tasmanian devils help keep their habitat clean.

Tasmanian devils are famous for their temper tantrums. When devils are bothered or threatened, their ears turn red, and they stomp their feet and bare their sharp teeth. They scream and snap their jaws, too. If their tantrums don't scare away an enemy, they create smelly fluids that make most animals run off. It's easy to see why this creature got its unfriendly name.

. . . .

1. **Why do Tasmanian devils hunt alone?**

   Ⓐ Their smell keeps other Tasmanian devils away.

   Ⓑ They travel faster by themselves.

   Ⓒ They are afraid of other Tasmanian devils.

   Ⓓ They don't want to share their food.

2. **Tasmanian devils probably got their name because _____.**

   Ⓐ they look like devils

   Ⓑ they have nasty tempers

   Ⓒ they eat dead animals

   Ⓓ they have sharp teeth

3. **If two Tasmanian devils saw each other, they would probably _____.**

   Ⓐ look for food together

   Ⓑ try to scare off other animals

   Ⓒ snap their jaws at one another

   Ⓓ ignore one another

4. **Tasmanian devils probably have strong jaws because _____.**

   Ⓐ they have big teeth

   Ⓑ they use them to build their homes

   Ⓒ they must scare off enemies

   Ⓓ they sometimes eat bones

Vo·cab·u·lar·y

A **prefix** is a word part that comes before a base word, word root, or other word part. A prefix changes a word's meaning.

The prefix **inter–** means "between" or "among."
The prefix **trans–** means "across."
The prefix **circum–** means "round" or "around."

Add the correct prefix from above to the beginning of each word part. Then write a sentence using the new word.

1. _____ continental = "across a continent"

   _____

2. _____ navigate = "to go entirely around something"

   _____

3. _____ stances = "the situations surrounding an event"

   _____

4. _____ national = "between nations"

   _____

5. _____ portation = "something that takes you across land or sea"

   _____

6. _____ val = "the period of time between two events"

   _____

7. _____ ference = "the outer boundary of a circular area"

   _____

© Evan-Moor Corp. • EMC 1066 • Daily Summer Activities

LANGUAGE LINES

Circle the coordinating conjunction or conjunctions in each sentence.

1. Let's choose a place to eat and a movie to see.

2. I would like to get pizza, but Emma just had pizza for lunch.

3. Emma thinks Mexican or Chinese food would be good.

4. Ella wants a hamburger and fries, yet she will eat anything.

5. Corey wants to get popcorn at the movies, so he won't eat much.

6. Tamara will only eat a salad, a sandwich, or fruit.

7. This is too complicated, so let's skip dinner and just go to the movie together.

8. We need to decide on a movie and a time to meet.

9. I want to see *Invaders* or *Cartoon Movie*, but Matt wants to see *Food Fight*!

10. We're all good friends, yet we can't agree on anything today!

In My Own Words

Think about the most interesting place you've been to. Explain why it was so interesting.

Mind Jigglers

Spoons and Forks

A. If you could use *only* a spoon or a fork for the rest of your life, which would you choose? Why?

_____

_____

B. What are five things that you could use a spoon or a fork for besides eating?

Spoon	Fork
1. _____	1. _____
2. _____	2. _____
3. _____	3. _____
4. _____	4. _____
5. _____	5. _____

C. Use the clues to find words that rhyme with either *spoon* or *fork*.

hangs in the night sky _____

a time to each lunch _____

ham or bacon _____

bottle stopper _____

in a little while _____

spun by a caterpillar _____

D. Myron is in charge of buying forks for the schoolwide spaghetti dinner. He bought 8 cartons of plastic forks. Each carton contains 12 boxes. Each box contains 72 forks. How many plastic forks did Myron buy?

_____ plastic forks

MATH TIME

Draw each line segment listed below, using a ruler or a straight edge. Then complete the sentence.

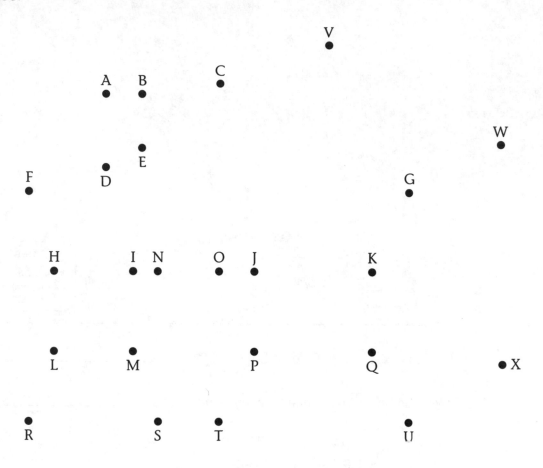

The line segments form a picture of a _____.

Line Segments

1. **RU**	8. **AD**	15. **NO**	22. **PQ**
2. **FG**	9. **FR**	16. **OT**	23. **JP**
3. **FC**	10. **GU**	17. **NT**	24. **CV**
4. **CG**	11. **HI**	18. **OS**	25. **GW**
5. **AB**	12. **IM**	19. **NS**	26. **VW**
6. **BE**	13. **LM**	20. **JK**	27. **WX**
7. **DE**	14. **HL**	21. **KQ**	28. **UX**

Geography

The Saint Lawrence Seaway

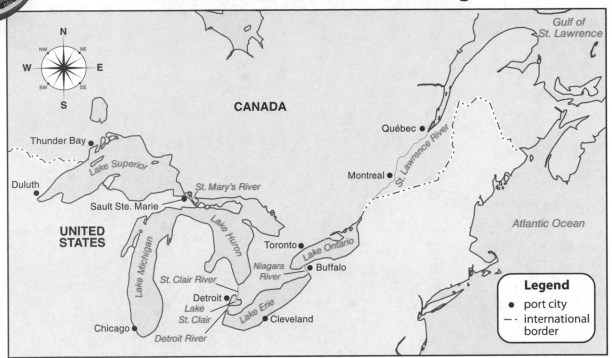

1. Which port city lies between Lake Erie and Lake Huron? _____

2. Which small lake on the Saint Lawrence Seaway is *not* _____
   a Great Lake?

3. Saint Lawrence Seaway is a major waterway that _____
   connects the Great Lakes to which ocean?

4. Name two port cities on the Saint Lawrence River. _____

5. Name the five Great Lakes.

   _____

   _____

6. Name the five rivers that help connect the Great Lakes.

   _____

   _____

WEEK 9

Check off each box as you complete the day's work.

Spelling Words

action

autobiography

automatic

bicycle

biography

biology

cyclone

enact

geology

photograph

portable

transport

Get Creative!

Turn this scribble into a pirate.

Write It Right

Rewrite each sentence and correct the errors.

1. the reporter askd do u plan to run for re-election mr president

_____

_____

2. the house shaked dishes rattled and the dog howled it was a earthquake!

_____

_____

3. rita bought her favorite book island of the blue dolphins on sale

_____

_____

MATH TIME

Complete the addition problems.

25	827	841	1,353
+ 91	+ 51	+ 259	+ 549

229	420	761	4,022
+ 77	+ 38	+ 219	+ 785

372	42	915	2,134
+ 28	+ 96	+ 222	+ 1,966

SPELL IT

Use these Greek and Latin word parts to help you make spelling words that fit each meaning.

bio = life	**geo** = earth	**cycle** = circle	**auto** = self	**logy** = study of	**bi** = two
port = carry	**act** = do	**photo** = light	**trans** = across	**graph** = write	

1. the study of the earth

   _____

2. a story you write about your own life

   _____

3. to carry something across a distance

   _____

4. to record using light

   _____

5. something that you do or complete

   _____

6. the study of living things

   _____

7. self-acting

   _____

8. able to be easily carried

   _____

9. a vehicle with two wheels

   _____

10. a rotating storm

    _____

11. a written account of someone else's life

    _____

12. to carry out or put into action

    _____

In My Own Words

Suppose you woke up one morning and were as small as a mouse. What are some advantages of your new size? What are some disadvantages?

_____

_____

_____

_____

_____

_____

LANGUAGE LINES

Independent clauses can stand alone as complete sentences.
Dependent clauses cannot stand alone.

Read each clause. Circle *independent* or *dependent*.

1.	while we were sleeping one night	independent	dependent
2.	a thunderstorm blew in from the north	independent	dependent
3.	rain pelted the windows of my bedroom	independent	dependent
4.	although I'm a sound sleeper	independent	dependent
5.	I awoke with a start	independent	dependent
6.	when I heard the first clap of thunder	independent	dependent
7.	since I had left the window open	independent	dependent
8.	my books on the windowsill are wet	independent	dependent

MATH TIME

Write *true* or *false* next to each math sentence.

< means *less than*	> means *greater than*
≤ means *less than or equal to*	≥ means *greater than or equal to*

1. $6.2 < 6.21$ _____

2. $4.5 \leq 4.51$ _____

3. $4.2 > 4.4$ _____

4. $2.1 \geq 2.5$ _____

5. $5.3 > 4.98$ _____

6. $2.3 \leq 2.30$ _____

7. $2.1 < 2.18$ _____

8. $4.0 > 4$ _____

9. $4.2 \geq 4.18$ _____

10. $5.1 > 5.6$ _____

Read the story. Then answer the questions.

Checking Out Giants

"Come on, Jesse! Let's find ourselves some giants!" yelled Max.

"Everything is giant here," said Jesse softly. "This place is huge." Oak and cypress trees greeted the boys as they started on a trail through the state park. The shady path was just wide enough for the two cousins to walk side by side.

Jesse enjoyed the peace and quiet after two hours of being in the car with Max. The only sound he heard was the occasional twitter of birds—until Max started complaining.

"We should have watched the Giants' baseball game instead of looking for a bunch of stupid, giant trees," Max said. Jesse ignored him and focused on the cool breeze and the smell of damp soil.

"Got any water, Jesse?" Max asked loudly, making Jesse jump. Jesse handed Max an extra bottle from his pack. Max took a swig and then squirted some water on Jesse, laughing. Jesse calmly wiped his face with his shirt and kept walking.

"Check out the size of this thing!" Max yelled. He was the first to spot the huge redwood tree blackened by lightning. Both boys stood at the base of the trunk, staring up.

"I don't think I can even see the top!" whispered Jesse.

Then the boys noticed that fire had carved out a large hollow space at the base of the trunk. They stooped to step through the opening. Inside the hole, they could barely see each other in the darkness.

Max grinned as he ran his hand down the rough interior bark. "We're *inside* a tree!" he exclaimed. "I admit it—this is way better than watching a ballgame!"

· ·

1. **Which part of the setting excited Max?**

   Ⓐ the inside of the redwood tree

   Ⓑ the shaded path

   Ⓒ the damp soil

   Ⓓ the car he and Jesse rode in

2. **How does Max show that he is unhappy?**

   Ⓐ He touches the inside of the redwood tree.

   Ⓑ He complains during the hike.

   Ⓒ He yells at Jesse.

   Ⓓ He walks down the path.

3. **Which of these is true about Jesse?**

   Ⓐ He is loud and lively.

   Ⓑ He is clumsy and careless.

   Ⓒ He is calm and quiet.

   Ⓓ He is slow and lazy.

4. **Which adjective best describes the setting?**

   Ⓐ peaceful

   Ⓑ dangerous

   Ⓒ noisy

   Ⓓ boring

Vo·cab·u·lar·y

A **blended word** combines two words into one. It usually begins with letters from one word and ends with letters from another. The first and second words' meanings combine to form the blended word's meaning.

gleam + sh**immer** = **glimmer**
The diamonds glimmer in the light.

Write the correct blended word from the box next to each equation below.

motel	smog	flurry	webcam
chortle	snazzy	clump	infomercial
videographer	fantabulous	emoticon	guesstimate

1. chunk + lump = _____

2. snappy + jazzy = _____

3. chuckle + snort = _____

4. smoke + fog = _____

5. guess + estimate = _____

6. video + photographer = _____

7. flutter + hurry = _____

8. fantastic + fabulous = _____

9. emotion + icon = _____

10. motor + hotel = _____

11. information + commercial = _____

12. World Wide Web + camera = _____

LANGUAGE LINES

Synonyms are two words that mean almost the same thing.

Choose the synonym in parentheses that best completes each sentence. Write the word on the line.

1. Maddy _____ longingly at the new baseball glove in the store.
   (gazed, watched)

2. This weekend was her chance to show what an _____ player she was.
   (enjoyable, excellent)

3. Maddy had practiced her _____ every day after school.
   (pitching, tossing)

4. She was getting better and better at _____ the ball, too.
   (capturing, catching)

5. Maddy was _____ in herself, but she was still nervous.
   (certain, confident)

6. She knew that the _____ mitt was just what she needed.
   (new, unused)

7. Maddy would _____ her mother tonight if she could buy it.
   (demand, ask)

In My Own Words

Your parents say you can go to camp this summer! Which type of camp would you choose—sports camp, computer camp, music camp, or another type? What would you hope to do there?

Mind Jigglers

Pizza Time

Three pizzas have been ordered for a pizza party. Each pizza has 10 slices. Each of the 15 guests gets 2 slices of pizza. Your job is to make sure that each guest gets 2 slices of pizza that he or she likes. You may give a guest 2 slices of the same pizza or of 2 different pizzas. Use numbers to show what kinds of pizza the guests will get. When you are done, every slice should be assigned to a guest. The first one has been done for you.

Pizza 1: Veggie Delight	**Pizza 2:** Pepperoni	**Pizza 3:** Ham and Pineapple
	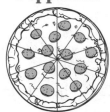	

Cassie will eat anything. ___1___ and ___2___	**Lila** is allergic to pepperoni. _____ and _____	**Jarid** is allergic to pineapple. _____ and _____
Kelly wants a lot of meat. _____ and _____	**Amber** does not like pepperoni. _____ and _____	**Olivia** likes pineapple and pepperoni. _____ and _____
Joshua loves pepperoni. _____ and _____	**Marcus** loves pepperoni. _____ and _____	**Chandra** likes ham but not pepperoni. _____ and _____
Micah does not eat ham. _____ and _____	**Solomon** does not like pepperoni. _____ and _____	**Benjamin** wants ham and pineapple. _____ and _____
Lucy loves vegetables. _____ and _____	**David** is a vegetarian. _____ and _____	**Tina** does not like vegetables. _____ and _____

MATH TIME

Data Sets

Use the rules below to help you complete the table.

To find the **range**, subtract the smallest number in a data set from the largest.

> **Data set: 3, 4, 5**
> **5 − 3 = 2**
> **The range is 2.**

If all the numbers in the set are the same, there is no range.

To find the **mean**, add all of the numbers in the set and divide by the number of items in the set.

> **Data set: 3, 5, 7**
> **3 + 5 + 7 = 15**
> **15 ÷ 3 = 5**
> **The mean is 5.**

To find the **median**, list the numbers in order from least to greatest. The middle number is the median.

> **Data set: 3, 5, 7**
> **The median is 5.**

If there is an even amount of numbers in the set, add the two numbers in the middle and divide their sum in half.

The number in a set that appears the most often is the **mode**.

> **3, 5, 7, 5, 9**
> **The mode is 5.**

If no number appears more than once, there is no mode.

Data Set	Range	Mean	Median	Mode
10, 14, 15, 15, 17				
3, 4, 6, 7, 7, 7, 8				
21, 21, 21, 21, 21				
30, 35, 40, 45, 50				
4, 5, 7, 9, 10, 10				

Geography

Regions of the United States

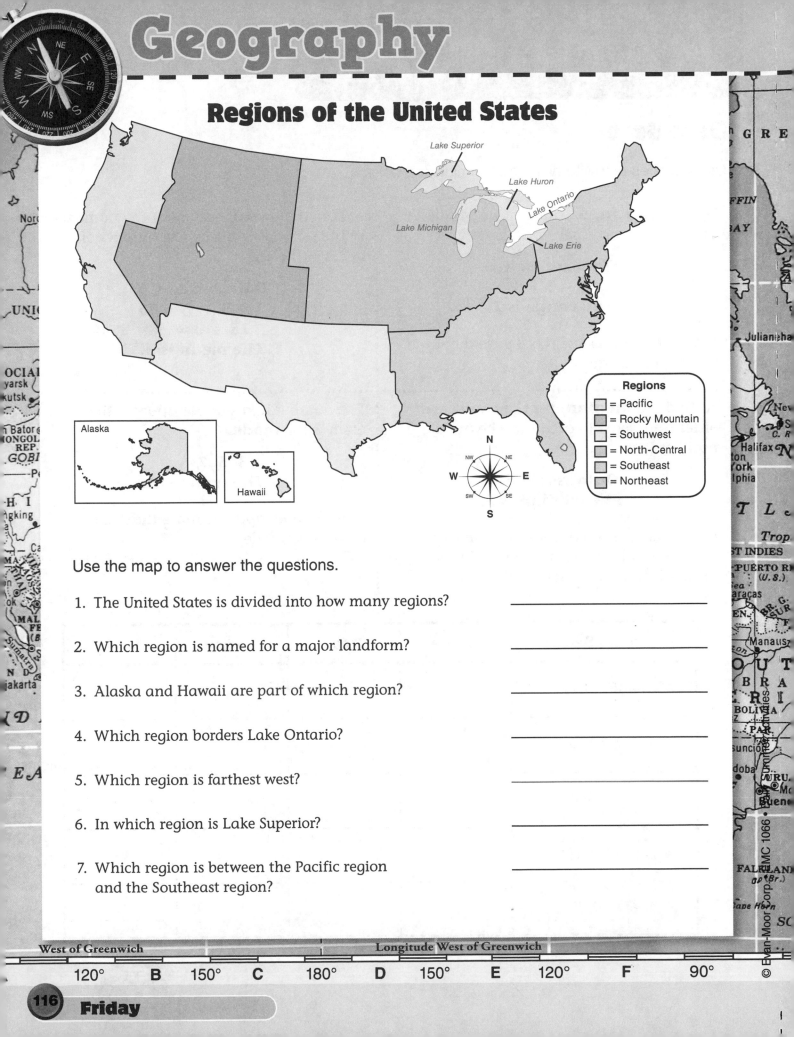

Use the map to answer the questions.

1. The United States is divided into how many regions? _____

2. Which region is named for a major landform? _____

3. Alaska and Hawaii are part of which region? _____

4. Which region borders Lake Ontario? _____

5. Which region is farthest west? _____

6. In which region is Lake Superior? _____

7. Which region is between the Pacific region and the Southeast region? _____

WEEK 10

Check off each box as you complete the day's work.

Spelling Words

agriculture

amphibian

atmosphere

characteristic

civilization

currency

environment

intersection

musician

representative

semicircle

substitute

Get Creative!

Draw a diagram of your room, using a bird's-eye view.

A Memorable Moment

What sticks in your mind about this week? Write about it.

_____

_____

_____

_____

_____

_____

Reading Record

	Book Title	Pages	Time
Monday			
Tuesday			
Wednesday			
Thursday			
Friday			

Describe a character you read about this week.

_____

_____

_____

_____

_____

Read the story. Then answer the questions.

The Brave Pioneer

I'm a smart and brave pioneer. At least that's what I thought when my family and I set out for our long trip west on the Oregon Trail. But then I learned otherwise.

On the first night on the trail, Ma and my sisters slept in the wagon. I slept next to the fire with Pa. But just as I dropped off to sleep, a cricket crawled across my forehead. I didn't sleep at all for the rest of the night.

"We slept fine in the wagon," said my sister in the morning.

I thought I was smart and brave, so on the second night, I slept outside again but wore my hat. Just as I dropped off to sleep, a mouse tickled my big toe. I didn't sleep at all for the rest of the night.

"We slept fine in the wagon," said my sister in the morning.

I thought I was smart and brave, so on the third night, I slept outside again but wore my boots. Just as I dropped off to sleep, a snake slithered across my hand. I didn't sleep at all for the rest of the night.

"We slept fine in the wagon," said my sister in the morning.

I thought I was smart and brave, so on the fourth night, I slept outside again but wore my gloves. Not a single creature touched my skin. But I was so hot that I didn't sleep at all that night. In the morning, I decided I'd rather be smart and well-rested than brave and tired.

"Don't worry, son," said Pa. "You'll have plenty of chances to be brave on this trip." Then he pointed to the map. "See? There are no bridges across any of these rivers."

· ·

1. **Where will the boy in the story most likely sleep on the fifth night?**

   Ⓐ in the wagon

   Ⓑ closer to the fire

   Ⓒ on top of his blankets

   Ⓓ in a puddle

2. **How did the boy probably feel on the morning after the fourth night?**

   Ⓐ tired

   Ⓑ brave

   Ⓒ smart

   Ⓓ cold

3. **If the boy had felt a tickle on his neck, he probably would have _____.**

   Ⓐ slept closer to the fire

   Ⓑ worn a scarf to bed

   Ⓒ gotten up and run

   Ⓓ woken his sister

4. **How will the boy be able to prove his bravery later in the story?**

   Ⓐ by sleeping inside

   Ⓑ by building a house

   Ⓒ by crossing a river without a bridge

   Ⓓ by guarding his mother and sisters

Write It Right

Rewrite the letter and correct the errors.

june 3 2012

dear uncle roberto

thank you so much four the birthday present ive wnted my own guitar for ages and the won you baught me is purfict youre the best

love
pedro

_____

_____

_____

_____

_____

_____

MATH TIME

Solve the problem below.

The school cafeteria offers the following menu each day. If a student picks one item from each category, how many different combinations can he order? _____

Choices for main dish:	Choices for side dish:	Choices for dessert:
• peanut butter-and-jelly sandwich • burrito • fish sticks	• vegetables • potatoes	• ice cream • brownie • cookies

SPELL IT

Fill in the missing syllables to make the spelling words for the week. Then count the number of syllables in each word and write the number in the box.

1. en _____ ron _____ ☐

2. agri _____ ture ☐

3. _____ rency ☐

4. _____ acter _____ tic ☐

5. mu _____ cian ☐

6. _____ icir _____ ☐

7. in _____ sec _____ ☐

8. repre _____ ta _____ ☐

9. _____ stitute ☐

10. _____ iliza _____ ☐

11. atmos _____ ☐

12. am _____ ian ☐

In My Own Words

Make up a new word. What does it mean? Use your new word in at least two sentences.

Vo·cab·u·lar·y

A **suffix** is a word part that comes after a base word or root.
A suffix changes a word's meaning and part of speech.

The suffixes **–able** and **–ible** form adjectives meaning "likely to," "can be," or "worthy of."
predict + **able** = predictable ("can be predicted")
reverse + **ible** = reversible ("can be reversed")

The suffixes **–ious** and **–ous** form adjectives meaning "full of" or "possessing the qualities of."
grace + **ious** = gracious ("full of grace")
venom + **ous** = venomous ("full of venom")

Answer each clue with a word that uses one of the suffixes above. If necessary, use a dictionary to help with spelling changes.

1. likely to be **adored** ___ ___ ___ ___ ___ ___ ___

2. full of **glamour** ___ ___ ___ ___ ___ ___ ___ ___

3. can be **avoided** ___ ___ ___ ___ ___ ___ ___ ___

4. full of **fury** ___ ___ ___ ___ ___ ___ ___

5. full of **danger** ___ ___ ___ ___ ___ ___ ___ ___

6. can be **accessed** ___ ___ ___ ___ ___ ___ ___ ___ ___

7. full of **anxiety** ___ ___ ___ ___ ___ ___ ___

8. can be **depended** upon ___ ___ ___ ___ ___ ___ ___ ___ ___

9. making good **sense** ___ ___ ___ ___ ___ ___ ___ ___

10. can be **chewed** ___ ___ ___ ___ ___ ___ ___ ___

11. can be **collected** ___ ___ ___ ___ ___ ___ ___ ___ ___ ___ ___

12. worthy of **admiring** ___ ___ ___ ___ ___ ___ ___ ___

© Evan-Moor Corp. • EMC 1066 • Daily Summer Activities

LANGUAGE LINES

Homophones are words that sound alike but have different spellings and meanings.

A. Circle the correct homophone to match the meaning.

Meaning		Homophone
1. how heavy something is	weight	wait
2. to put down on paper	right	write
3. belonging to them	they're	their
4. to make a harsh sound	groan	grown
5. in this place	here	hear
6. a piece of wood	bored	board

B. Write a sentence for each of these homophones.

Through: _____

Threw: _____

In My Own Words

You have decided to volunteer to help your community. What would you choose to do? Why?

Mind Jigglers

Punchline

Find the hidden joke and its answer. Read the directions below and use them to cross off words in both tables. Then read the remaining words from left to right. Write the joke and its answer on the lines.

- In each row, cross off the word that comes first in alphabetical order.
- Cross off any word with the pattern *consonant, vowel, consonant, vowel, consonant.*
- Cross off the words that are three letters or longer and that make other words if you write them backward.
- Cross off the names of colors.
- Cross off the adjectives beginning with *B* or *T*.
- Cross off the words with *Q* in them.
- Cross off the compound words.

Joke

indigo	power	what	happy	terrific	ton
happened	sunshine	cat	to	caves	pets
bear	beautiful	solar	mauve	the	quart
man	igloo	who	paper	into	stayed
made	super	pot	up	magenta	quack
all	faded	night	terrible	add	big
quiver	teal	playful	salad	wondering	quiz
where	hide	queen	homework	tan	the
absent	amber	sun	spit	polar	tiny
boring	reed	boat	went	bold	outside

_____

_____

Answers

quest	it	file	makeup	finally	keyhole
tacky	beast	dawned	beige	without	on
sales	popcorn	hide	him	loop	quit

_____

MATH TIME

Mystery Shape

Draw a sketch of each of the following polygons using the clues given. Label the length of each side of the polygon. The first one has been done for you.

> **Remember:**
>
> ⌐→ A right angle forms a square corner.
>
> ∠→ An acute angle is less than a right angle.
>
> **Prime numbers** can be divided only by 1 and themselves.
> **Congruent** means having the same length and same angles.

1. This polygon has the following characteristics:
   - It has a perimeter of 12 inches.
   - It has four equal sides.
   - It has four right angles.

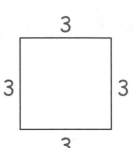

2. This polygon has the following characteristics:
   - It has a perimeter of 18 centimeters.
   - It has four sides.
   - It has four right angles.
   - It has two sides that are each 5 centimeters longer than each of the other sides.

3. This polygon has the following characteristics:
   - It has a perimeter of 16 inches.
   - It has no right angles.
   - It has four sides.
   - The lengths of all the sides are prime numbers.
   - The lengths of the sides are odd numbers.
   - There are two pairs of congruent, parallel sides.

4. This polygon has the following characteristics:
   - It has a perimeter of 7.5 centimeters.
   - It has three acute angles.
   - It has three sides.
   - The three sides are equal in length.

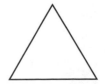

Geography

Central America

Map labels
- Belize
- Belmopan
- Mexico
- Guatemala
- Guatemala City
- Honduras
- Tegucigalpa
- San Salvador
- El Salvador
- Nicaragua
- Managua
- Caribbean Sea
- Costa Rica
- San José
- Pacific Ocean
- Panama City
- Panama
- South America

Key
⬟ national capital

Compass: N, NW, NE, W, E, SW, SE, S

1. How many countries make up Central America? _____

2. Which waterways border Central America?

_____

3. Which country does *not* border the Caribbean Sea? _____

4. Name the capital city of each country in Central America.

Belize: _____ Guatemala: _____

Honduras: _____ El Salvador: _____

Nicaragua: _____ Costa Rica: _____

Panama: _____

© Evan-Moor Corp. • EMC 1066 • Daily Summer Activities

Answer Key

Checking your child's work is an important part of learning. It allows you to see what your child knows well and what areas need more practice. It also provides an opportunity for you to help your child understand that making mistakes is a part of learning.

The answer key pages can be used in several ways:

➤ Remove the answer pages and give the book to your child. Go over the answers with him or her as each day's work is completed.

➤ Leave the answer pages in the book and give the practice pages to your child one day at a time.

➤ Leave the answer pages in the book so your child can check his or her own work as the pages are completed. It is still important to review the pages with your child if you use this method.

Page 11

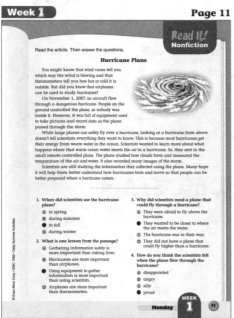

Page 12

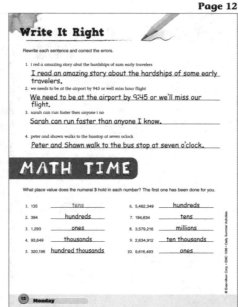

Page 13

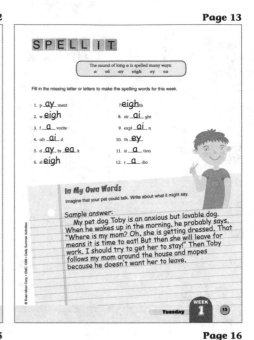

Page 14

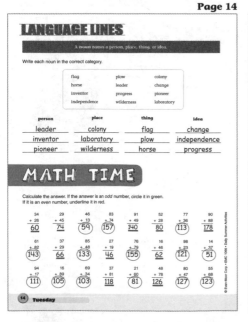

Page 15

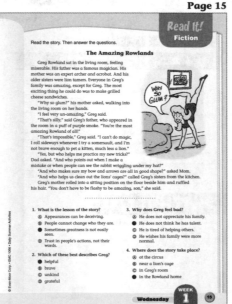

Page 16

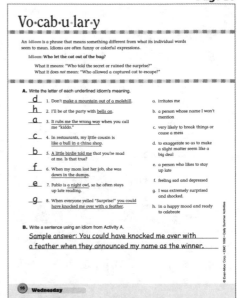

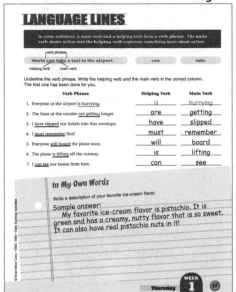

LANGUAGE LINES

In some sentences, a main verb and a helping verb form a verb phrase. The main verb shows action and the helping verb expresses something more about action.

verb phrase
Maria **can take** a taxi to the airport.   can   take
helping verb   main verb

Underline the verb phrase. Write the helping verb and the main verb in the correct column. The first one has been done for you.

Verb Phrase	Helping Verb	Main Verb
1. Everyone at the airport <u>is hurrying</u>.	is	hurrying
2. The lines at the counter <u>are getting</u> longer.	are	getting
3. I <u>have slipped</u> our tickets into this envelope.	have	slipped
4. I <u>must remember</u> that!	must	remember
5. Everyone <u>will board</u> the plane soon.	will	board
6. The plane <u>is lifting</u> off the runway.	is	lifting
7. I <u>can see</u> our house from here.	can	see

In My Own Words

Write a description of your favorite ice-cream flavor.

Sample answer:
My favorite ice-cream flavor is pistachio. It is green and has a creamy, nutty flavor that is so sweet. It can also have real pistachio nuts in it!

Thursday **1** 17

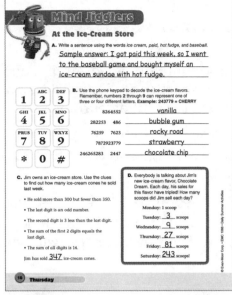

Mind Jigglers

At the Ice-Cream Store

A. Write a sentence using the words *ice cream, paid, hot fudge,* and *baseball.*

Sample answer: I got paid this week, so I went to the baseball game and bought myself an ice-cream sundae with hot fudge.

ABC 2	DEF 3
1	
GHI 4	JKL 5	MNO 6
PRUS 7	TUV 8	WXYZ 9
*	0	#

B. Use the phone keypad to decode the ice-cream flavors. Remember, numbers 2 through 9 can represent one of three or four different letters. Example: 243779 = CHERRY

8264552	vanilla
282253 486	bubble gum
76259 7623	rocky road
7872923779	strawberry
246265283 2447	chocolate chip

C. Jim owns an ice-cream store. Use the clues to find out how many ice-cream cones he sold last week.

• He sold more than 300 but fewer than 350.
• The last digit is an odd number.
• The second digit is 3 less than the last digit.
• The sum of the first 2 digits equals the last digit.
• The sum of all digits is 14.

Jim has sold **347** ice-cream cones.

D. Everybody is talking about Jim's new ice-cream flavor, Chocolate Dream. Each day, his sales for this flavor have tripled! How many scoops did Jim sell each day?

Monday:	1 scoop
Tuesday:	**3** scoops
Wednesday:	**9** scoops
Thursday:	**27** scoops
Friday:	**81** scoops
Saturday:	**243** scoops!

18 Thursday

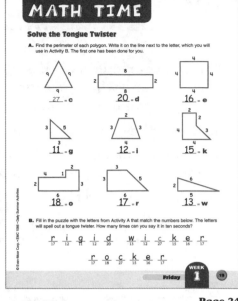

MATH TIME

Solve the Tongue Twister

A. Find the perimeter of each polygon. Write it on the line next to the letter, which you will use in Activity B. The first one has been done for you.

<u>27</u> = c   <u>20</u> = d   <u>16</u> = e

<u>11</u> = g   <u>12</u> = i   <u>15</u> = k

<u>18</u> = o   <u>17</u> = r   <u>13</u> = w

B. Fill in the puzzle with the letters from Activity A that match the numbers below. The letters will spell out a tongue twister. How many times can you say it in ten seconds?

r i g i d   w i c k e r
17   15   16   17

r o c k e r
17   15   16   17

Friday **1** 19

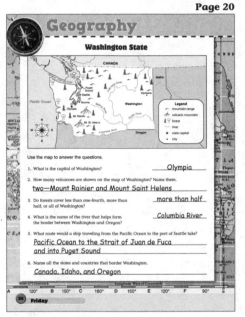

Geography

Washington State

Use the map to answer the questions.

1. What is the capital of Washington? **Olympia**

2. How many volcanoes are shown on the map of Washington? Name them.
two—Mount Rainier and Mount Saint Helens

3. Do forests cover less than one-fourth, more than half, or all of Washington? **more than half**

4. What is the name of the river that helps form the border between Washington and Oregon? **Columbia River**

5. What route would a ship traveling from the Pacific Ocean to the port of Seattle take?
Pacific Ocean to the Strait of Juan de Fuca and into Puget Sound

6. Name all the states and countries that border Washington.
Canada, Idaho, and Oregon

20 Friday

A 120° B 150° C 180° D 150° E 120° F 90°

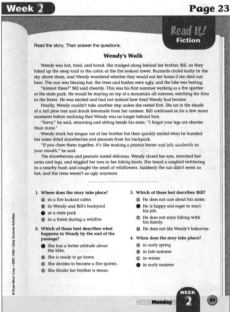

Read It! Fiction

Read the story. Then answer the questions.

Wendy's Walk

Wendy was hot, tired, and bored. She trudged along behind her brother, Bill, as they hiked up the steep trail to the cabin at the fire lookout tower. Buzzards circled lazily in the sky above them, and Wendy wondered whether they would eat her bones if she died out here. The sun was blazing hot, the trees and bushes were ugly, and the hike was boring.

"Almost there!" Bill said cheerily. This was his first summer working as a fire spotter at the state park. He would be staying on top of a mountain all summer, watching for fires in the forest. He was excited and had not noticed how tired Wendy had become.

Finally, Wendy couldn't take another step unless she rested first. She sat in the shade of a tall pine tree and drank lemonade from her canteen. Bill continued on for a few more moments before realizing that Wendy was no longer behind him.

"Sorry," he said, returning and sitting beside his sister. "I forgot your legs are shorter than mine."

Wendy stuck her tongue out at her brother but then quickly smiled when he handed her some dried strawberries and peanuts from his backpack.

"If you chew them together, it's like making a peanut butter and jelly sandwich in your mouth," he said.

The strawberries and peanuts tasted delicious. Wendy closed her eyes, stretched her arms and legs, and wiggled her toes in her hiking boots. She heard a songbird twittering in a nearby bush and caught the smell of wildflowers. Suddenly the sun didn't seem so hot, and the trees weren't so ugly anymore.

1. Where does the story take place?
Ⓐ in a fire lookout cabin
Ⓑ in Wendy and Bill's backyard
● at a state park
Ⓓ in a forest during a wildfire

2. Which of these best describes what happens to Wendy by the end of the passage?
● She has a better attitude about the hike.
Ⓑ She is ready to go home.
Ⓒ She decides to become a fire spotter.
Ⓓ She thinks her brother is mean.

3. Which of these best describes Bill?
Ⓐ He does not care about his sister.
● He is happy and eager to start his job.
Ⓒ He does not enjoy hiking with his family.
Ⓓ He does not like Wendy's behavior.

4. When does the story take place?
Ⓐ in early spring
Ⓑ in late summer
Ⓒ in winter
● in early summer

Monday **2** 23

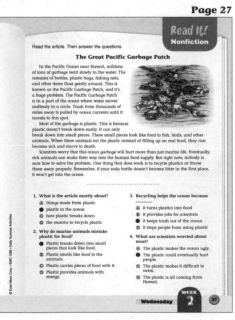

Write It Right

Rewrite each sentence and correct the errors.

1. please put a ice cube in there lemonade
Please put an ice cube in their lemonade.

2. does the music start at 400 or 430 inquired Ms Clark
"Does the music start at 4:00 or 4:30?" inquired Ms. Clark.

3. the workmen has come to repair the roof on hermans house
The workmen have come (or The workman has come) to repair the roof on Herman's house.

4. wood you put these groceries away emily her mom asked
"Would you put these groceries away, Emily?" her mom asked.

MATH TIME

Complete the division problems. Note the remainder when appropriate.

6 / 4)24	8 / 4)32	9 r 4 / 5)49	6 r 4 / 9)58	3 r 5 / 8)29

7 r 1 / 2)15	16 r 4 / 5)84	5 r 5 / 6)35	3 r 3 / 8)27	11 r 1 / 2)23

3 r 4 / 7)25	7 r 6 / 8)62	5 / 4)20	7 / 6)42	16 r 1 / 5)81

24 Monday

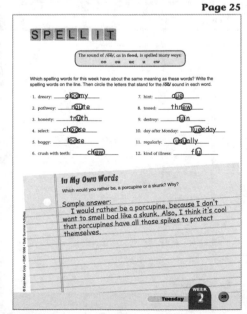

SPELL IT

The sound of /ōō/, as in *food,* is spelled many ways:
oo   ou   ue   ew

Which spelling words for this week have about the same meaning as these words? Write the spelling words on the line. Then circle the letters that stand for the /ōō/ sound in each word.

1. dreary: gl**oo**my
2. pathway: r**ou**te
3. honesty: tr**u**th
4. select: ch**oo**se
5. baggy: l**oo**se
6. crush with teeth: ch**ew**

7. hint: cl**ue**
8. tossed: thr**ew**
9. destroy: r**ui**n
10. day after Monday: T**ue**sday
11. regularly: us**ua**lly
12. kind of illness: fl**u**

In My Own Words

Which would you rather be, a porcupine or a skunk? Why?

Sample answer:
I would rather be a porcupine, because I don't want to smell bad like a skunk. Also, I think it's cool that porcupines have all those spikes to protect themselves.

Tuesday **2** 25

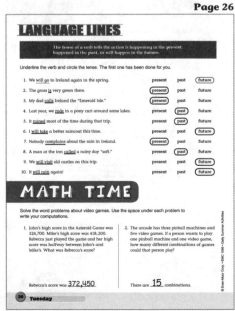

LANGUAGE LINES

The tense of a verb tells the action is happening in the present, the past, or will happen in the future.

Underline the verb and circle the tense. The first one has been done for you.

1. We <u>will go</u> to Ireland again in the spring. present past (future)
2. The grass <u>is</u> very green there. (present) past future
3. My dad <u>calls</u> Ireland the "Emerald Isle." (present) past future
4. Last year, we <u>rode</u> in a pony cart around some lakes. present (past) future
5. It <u>rained</u> most of the time during that trip. present (past) future
6. I <u>will take</u> a better raincoat this time. present past (future)
7. Nobody <u>complains</u> about the rain in Ireland. (present) past future
8. A man at the inn <u>called</u> a rainy day "soft." present (past) future
9. We <u>will visit</u> old castles on this trip. present past (future)
10. It <u>will rain</u> again! present past (future)

MATH TIME

Solve the word problems about video games. Use the space under each problem to write your computations.

1. John's high score in the Asteroid Game was 326,700. Mike's high score was 418,200. Rebecca just played the game and her high score was halfway between John's and Mike's. What was Rebecca's score?

Rebecca's score was **372,450**

2. The arcade has three pinball machines and five video games. If a person wants to play one pinball machine and one video game, how many different combinations of games could that person play?

There are **15** combinations.

26 Tuesday

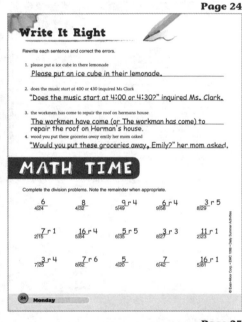

Read It! Nonfiction

Read the article. Then answer the questions.

The Great Pacific Garbage Patch

In the Pacific Ocean near Hawaii, millions of tons of garbage swirl slowly in the water. The remains of bottles, plastic bags, fishing nets, and other items float gently around. This is known as the Pacific Garbage Patch. The Pacific Garbage Patch is in a part of the ocean where water moves endlessly in a circle. Trash from thousands of miles away is pulled by ocean currents until it travels to this spot.

Most of the garbage is plastic. This is because plastic doesn't break down easily. It can only break down into small pieces. These small pieces look like food to fish, birds, and other animals. When these animals eat the plastic instead of filling up on real food, they can become sick and starve to death.

Scientists worry that this ocean garbage will hurt more than just marine life. Eventually, sick animals can make their way into the human food supply. But right now, nobody is sure how to solve the problem. One thing that does work is to recycle plastics or throw them away properly. Remember, if your soda bottle doesn't become litter in the first place, it won't get into the ocean.

1. What is the article mostly about?
Ⓐ things made from plastic
● plastic in the ocean
Ⓒ how plastic breaks down
Ⓓ the reasons to recycle plastic

2. Why do marine animals mistake plastic for food?
● Plastic breaks down into small pieces that look like food.
Ⓑ Plastic smells like food to the animals.
Ⓒ Plastic carries pieces of food with it.
Ⓓ Plastic provides animals with energy.

3. Recycling helps the ocean because
Ⓐ it turns plastics into food
Ⓑ it provides jobs for scientists
● it keeps trash out of the ocean
Ⓓ it stops people from using plastic

4. What are scientists worried about most?
Ⓐ The plastic makes the ocean ugly.
● The plastic could eventually hurt people.
Ⓒ The plastic makes it difficult to swim.
Ⓓ The plastic is all coming from Hawaii.

Wednesday **2** 27

Vo·cab·u·lar·y

Using precise language makes your meaning clear and your writing more interesting. Choose carefully among synonyms to make your writing precise.

For example, when you write about a sound, you can use specific words to describe that sound.

I quietly closed the door with a click.
Jane slammed the door shut in anger.

Write the word from the box that matches the sound being described in each sentence.

| fizz | glug | clang | sizzle | rustle |
| flap | drip | chime | rumble | crackle |

1. This sound can be made when oil hits a hot pan. — **sizzle**
2. This sound can be made when you pour a soft drink. — **fizz**
3. This sound can be made by a large car engine. — **rumble**
4. This sound can be made by leaves blowing in the wind. — **rustle**
5. This sound can be made by wood burning in a campfire. — **crackle**
6. This sound can be made by a metal spoon hitting a pot. — **clang**
7. This sound can be made by a bird moving its wings. — **flap**
8. This sound can be made by a leaky faucet. — **drip**
9. This sound can be made by water going down a drain. — **glug**
10. This sound can be made by a doorbell. — **chime**

28 Wednesday

LANGUAGE LINES

The words *lie* and *lay* are often confused. Use *lie* to mean "to rest or recline." Use *lay* to mean "to put or place."

Write the correct word—either *lie* or *lay*—to complete each sentence.

1. Before I **lie** down, I should organize my desk.
2. First, I will **lay** my CDs on my desk next to my computer.
3. My papers are scattered around, so I will gather them and **lay** them in a stack.
4. Next, I will **lay** my schoolbooks next to the papers.
5. While I am organizing, my cat decides to **lie** on top of my computer!
6. I pick her up and **lay** her on the bed.
7. I watch my cat **lay** her paws across my pillow.
8. After a few more minutes, I **lie** down with her for a nice nap.

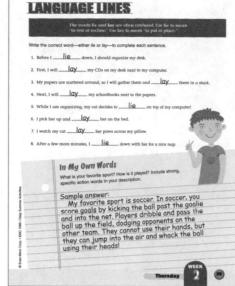

In My Own Words

What is your favorite sport? How is it played? Include strong, specific action words in your description.

Sample answer:
My favorite sport is soccer. In soccer, you score goals by kicking the ball past the goalie and into the net. Players dribble and pass the ball up the field, dodging opponents on the other team. They cannot use their hands, but they can jump into the air and whack the ball using their heads!

Thursday WEEK 2 29

Mind Jigglers

Picture This

Write the familiar phrase that each clue illustrates. The first one is done for you.

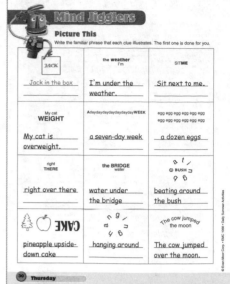

JACK	the **weather** I'm	SITME
Jack in the box	I'm under the weather.	Sit next to me.
My cat **WEIGHT**	AdaydaydaydaydaydayWEEK	egg egg egg egg egg egg egg egg egg egg
My cat is overweight.	a seven-day week	a dozen eggs
right **THERE**	the **BRIDGE** water	a l / ⊕ BUSH 9 B
right over there	water under the bridge	beating around the bush
🌲🍎 **CAKE**	h a n g i n g	The cow jumped the moon
pineapple upside-down cake	hanging around	The cow jumped over the moon.

30 Thursday

MATH TIME

Fruit Pie

Read the pie chart below. Next, answer the questions using the chart on the right. Then write the letter of the correct answer next to the question. The letters will spell out the name of a popular fruit drink.

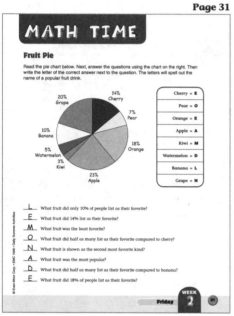

20% Grape
14% Cherry
7% Pear
10% Banana
5% Watermelon
3% Kiwi
18% Orange
23% Apple

| Cherry = E |
| Pear = O |
| Orange = E |
| Apple = A |
| Kiwi = M |
| Watermelon = D |
| Banana = L |
| Grape = N |

L What fruit did only 10% of people list as their favorite?
E What fruit was the least favorite?
M What fruit is shown as the second most favorite kind?
O What fruit did half as many list as their favorite compared to cherry?
N What fruit was the most popular?
A What fruit did half as many list as their favorite compared to banana?
D What fruit did 18% of people list as their favorite?

Friday WEEK 2 31

Geography

Latitude and Longitude

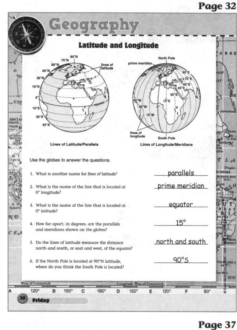

Lines of Latitude/Parallels
Lines of Longitude/Meridians

Use the globes to answer the questions.

1. What is another name for *lines of latitude*? — **parallels**
2. What is the name of the line that is located at 0° longitude? — **prime meridian**
3. What is the name of the line that is located at 0° latitude? — **equator**
4. How far apart, in degrees, are the parallels and meridians shown on the globes? — **15°**
5. Do the lines of latitude measure the distance north and south, or east and west, of the equator? — **north and south**
6. If the North Pole is located at 90°N latitude, where do you think the South Pole is located? — **90°S**

32 Friday

Read the article. Then answer the questions.

Read It! Nonfiction

Brain Freeze

Have you ever eaten ice cream on a hot day and suddenly felt a sharp pain in your head? If so, you have had a very common experience that some people call a "brain freeze."

Brain freezes are caused when cold food or liquid touches the roof of your mouth. Nerves in your mouth send a signal to your brain. Your brain then turns the signal into a sharp pain. However, the pain does not go to your mouth where the cold is—it stays in your head.

Most brain freezes last for less than 30 seconds. But if you want to make it go away quicker, you can try a couple of tricks. When you start to get a brain freeze, push your tongue against the roof of your mouth. This sometimes warms up your mouth so that the nerves don't send the signal that causes a headache. You can also try preventing brain freezes from the start by eating and drinking more slowly. If you take smaller bites or sips and wait longer between them, your mouth won't get as cold. Of course, sometimes a cold drink or an ice-cream cone on a hot day is just too good to enjoy slowly!

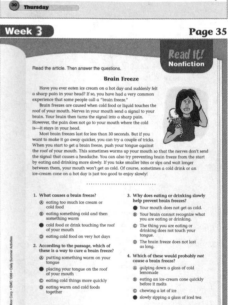

1. What causes a brain freeze?
   Ⓐ eating too much ice cream or cold food
   Ⓑ breathing cold air and then something warm
   ● cold food or drink touching the roof of your mouth
   Ⓓ eating cold food on very hot days

2. According to the passage, which of these is a way to cure a brain freeze?
   Ⓐ putting something warm on your tongue
   ● placing your tongue on the roof of your mouth
   Ⓒ eating cold things more quickly
   Ⓓ eating warm and cold foods together

3. Why does eating or drinking slowly help prevent brain freezes?
   ● Your mouth does not get as cold.
   Ⓑ Your brain cannot recognize what you are eating or drinking.
   Ⓒ The thing you are eating or drinking does not touch your tongue.
   Ⓓ The brain freeze does not last as long.

4. Which of these would probably *not* cause a brain freeze?
   Ⓐ gulping down a glass of cold lemonade
   Ⓑ eating an ice-cream cone quickly before it melts
   Ⓒ chewing a lot of ice
   ● slowly sipping a glass of iced tea

Monday WEEK 3 35

Write It Right

Rewrite each sentence and correct the errors.

1. mavis ate most of her salad but she left an orange slice
   Mavis ate most of her salad, but she left an orange slice.
2. dr conrads wife jill will join him at the ceremony
   Dr. Conrad's wife, Jill, will join him at the ceremony.
3. was the musicians nervous before the concert begun
   Was the musician nervous (or Were the musicians nervous) before the concert began?
4. mr matthews told jake that he shuld go to the principles office
   Mr. Matthews told Jake that he should go to the principal's office.

MATH TIME

Complete the problems. Two of them have been done for you.

$\frac{4}{5} + \frac{1}{5} = \frac{5}{5} = 1$ $\frac{1}{4} + \frac{1}{2} = \frac{3}{4}$
$3\frac{1}{4} + 1\frac{3}{4} = 5$ $5\frac{5}{6} + 2\frac{1}{6} = \frac{17}{3} \cdot \frac{7}{3} \cdot \frac{24}{3} \cdot \frac{1}{3} = 8$
$3\frac{1}{4} + 1\frac{1}{4} = 5\frac{1}{2}$ $4 + \frac{1}{4} = 4\frac{1}{4}$
$1\frac{1}{2} + 3\frac{1}{4} = 4\frac{3}{4}$ $3\frac{1}{2} + \frac{1}{2} = 4$
$2\frac{1}{2} + 3\frac{1}{5} = 5\frac{7}{10}$ $3\frac{1}{3} + 1\frac{2}{3} = 5\frac{1}{12}$
$3\frac{4}{5} + 5\frac{1}{3} = 9\frac{2}{15}$ $4\frac{1}{3} + 1\frac{5}{5} = 6\frac{1}{3}$

36 Monday

SPELL IT

Spell words with endings:
-ed -ing -est

Add the ending to each base word to correctly write the spelling words for the week. Remember that the spelling of some words will change when the endings are added.

Add –ing		Add –ed		Add –est	
ski	**skiing**	study	**studied**	quick	**quickest**
excite	**exciting**	carry	**carried**	tiny	**tiniest**
exist	**existing**	surround	**surrounded**	lonely	**loneliest**
trade	**trading**	finish	**finished**		
swim	**swimming**				

In My Own Words

Imagine you had a swimming pool full of jelly. What would you do with it? Be creative.

Sample answer:
I would invite my friends Peanut Butter and Fluff over for a swim. We would float across the jelly on huge slices of bread while sipping our glasses of milk.

Tuesday WEEK 3 37

LANGUAGE LINES

Adverbs modify verbs, adjectives, and other adverbs. Adverbs can tell when, where, and how something is happening.

A. Circle the adverb in each sentence.

1. (Soon) we arrived at the aquarium.
2. We clapped and cheered (loudly).
3. Someone was waiting for us (outside).
4. We (eagerly) left the bus.

B. Does the underlined adverb tell *when*, *where*, or *how*? Circle the correct answer.

1. We *excitedly* walked to the entrance.   when   where   (how)
2. The otters swam *nearby*.   when   (where)   how
3. A guide *quietly* talked to us about otters.   when   where   (how)
4. *Then* it was feeding time.   (when)   where   how
5. The otters waited *patiently* for their supper.   when   where   (how)

MATH TIME

Solve the word problems about recycling.

1. Tim's family was collecting aluminum cans to recycle. They found out that they would get two cents for every three cans they collected. If they collected 2,187 cans, how much money did they receive?
   Answer: **$14.58**

2. Bettler Elementary School was recycling their paper. They found that when they filled a barrel with paper, it weighed an average of 463 pounds. If they collected 16 barrels of paper during the year, what was the approximate weight of the paper?
   Answer: **7,408 lbs**

38 Tuesday

Answer Key 131

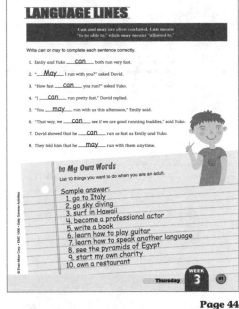

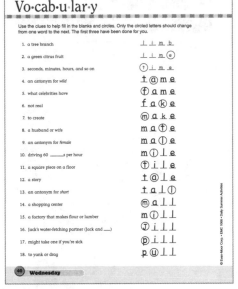

Page 39

Read It! Nonfiction

Read one person's opinion of Lake Tahoe. Then answer the questions.

The Lake on Top of a Mountain

Imagine a lake as blue as the summer sky, surrounded by thousands of pine trees and towering mountains. It sounds like something from a storybook, but Lake Tahoe is a real place in the Sierra Nevada mountains, along the border of California and Nevada.

People come during every season to enjoy Lake Tahoe. It is the perfect spot for camping, boating, fishing, biking, and hiking. However, Lake Tahoe is best known for its snow sports. Most of the small towns surrounding Lake Tahoe have lodges where families can go to ski or snowboard. These resorts are much more fun to stay at than the ones in other parts of the country.

Thousands of people visit Lake Tahoe each year, but the area was popular long before California and Nevada were even states. Native Americans from the Washoe (WASH-oh) tribe traveled through the mountains and spent their summers at Lake Tahoe. In fact, the name Tahoe comes from a Washoe word meaning "big water." The Washoe were expert hunters who used the land and water for their food supply. They even created many legends about the lake. The best one is about a giant birdlike monster that lived in the middle of the lake and ate people!

While people now use Lake Tahoe mostly for fun rather than survival, it is still important to keep the water and land clean. California and Nevada work together to make sure these natural resources are used wisely. It would be terrible if the lake and mountains became too polluted for everyone to enjoy. There is no place as beautiful or fun for a vacation as Lake Tahoe.

1. Which one is an opinion about the ski resorts in Lake Tahoe?
- ● They are more fun than other ski resorts.
- ○ Many towns around the lake have resorts.
- ○ The resorts are popular during the winter.
- ○ Families can stay at the resorts.

2. Which one of these is an opinion?
- ○ The Washoe tribe spent summers at Lake Tahoe.
- ● It would be terrible if Lake Tahoe became too dirty for people to enjoy.
- ○ People come to fish on Lake Tahoe.
- ○ Lake Tahoe is surrounded by pine trees.

3. Which one is a fact about Lake Tahoe?
- ○ It is a perfect spot for camping.
- ○ Its resorts are fun to stay at.
- ○ It is better for snow sports than water sports.
- ● It borders California and Nevada.

4. Which one is an opinion about the Washoe?
- ○ They created many legends.
- ○ They hunted for their food.
- ○ They traveled through the mountains.
- ● Their best legend is about a bird monster.

Wednesday — WEEK 3 — 39

Page 40

Vo·cab·u·lar·y

Use the clues to help fill in the blanks and circles. Only the circled letters should change from one word to the next. The first three have been done for you.

1. a tree branch — l i m b
2. a green citrus fruit — l i m e
3. seconds, minutes, hours, and so on — t i m e
4. an antonym for wild — t a m e
5. what celebrities have — f a m e
6. not real — f a k e
7. to create — m a k e
8. a husband or wife — m a t e
9. an antonym for female — m a l e
10. driving 60 ___ s per hour — m i l e
11. a square piece on a floor — t i l e
12. a story — t a l e
13. an antonym for short — t a l l
14. a shopping center — m a l l
15. a factory that makes flour or lumber — m i l l
16. Jack's water-fetching partner (Jack and ___) — J i l l
17. might take one if you're sick — p i l l
18. to yank or drag — p u l l

40 — Wednesday

Page 41

LANGUAGE LINES

Can and may are often confused. Can means "to be able to," while may means "allowed to."

Write can or may to complete each sentence correctly.

1. Emily and Yuko __can__ both run very fast.
2. "__May__ I run with you?" asked David.
3. "How fast __can__ you run?" asked Yuko.
4. "I __can__ run pretty fast," David replied.
5. "You __may__ run with us this afternoon," Emily said.
6. "That way, we __can__ see if we are good running buddies," said Yuko.
7. David showed that he __can__ run as fast as Emily and Yuko.
8. They told him that he __may__ run with them anytime.

In My Own Words

List 10 things you want to do when you are an adult.

Sample answer:
1. go to Italy
2. go sky diving
3. surf in Hawaii
4. become a professional actor
5. write a book
6. learn how to play guitar
7. learn how to speak another language
8. see the pyramids of Egypt
9. start my own charity
10. own a restaurant

Thursday — WEEK 3 — 41

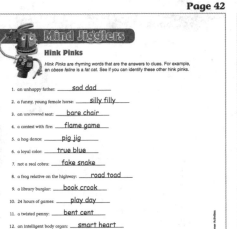

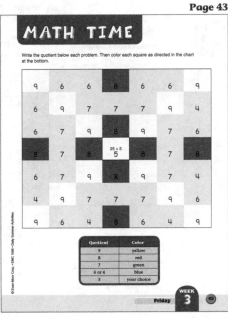

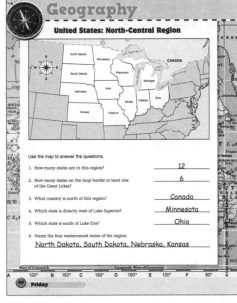

Page 42

Mind Jigglers

Hink Pinks

Hink Pinks are rhyming words that are the answers to clues. For example, an *obese feline* is a *fat cat*. See if you can identify these other hink pinks.

1. an unhappy father — sad dad
2. a funny, young female horse — silly filly
3. an uncovered seat — bare chair
4. a contest with fire — flame game
5. a hog dance — pig jig
6. a loyal color — true blue
7. not a real cobra — fake snake
8. a frog relative on the highway — road toad
9. a library burglar — book crook
10. 24 hours of games — play day
11. a twisted penny — bent cent
12. an intelligent body organ — smart heart
13. an orca prison — whale jail
14. a hilarious rabbit — funny bunny
15. 50 percent of a giggle — half laugh
16. an ill young chicken — sick chick

42 — Thursday

Page 43

MATH TIME

Write the quotient below each problem. Then color each square as directed in the chart at the bottom.

Quotient	Color
9	yellow
8	red
7	green
6 or 4	blue
5	your choice

Friday — WEEK 3 — 43

Page 44

Geography

United States: North-Central Region

Use the map to answer the questions.

1. How many states are in this region? — 12
2. How many states on the map border at least one of the Great Lakes? — 6
3. What country is north of this region? — Canada
4. Which state is directly west of Lake Superior? — Minnesota
5. Which state is south of Lake Erie? — Ohio
6. Name the four westernmost states of the region.
North Dakota, South Dakota, Nebraska, Kansas

44 — Friday

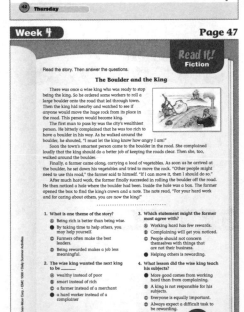

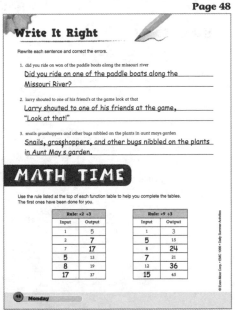

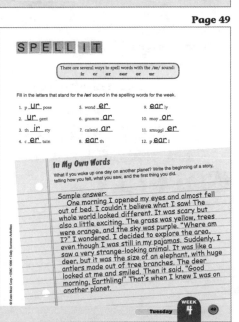

Week 4 — Page 47

Read It! Fiction

Read the story. Then answer the questions.

The Boulder and the King

There was once a wise king who was ready to stop being the king. So he ordered some workers to roll a large boulder onto the road that led through town. Then the king hid nearby and watched to see if anyone would move the huge rock from its place in the road. This person would become king.

The first man to pass by was the city's wealthiest person. He bitterly complained that he was too rich to have a boulder in his way. As he walked around the boulder, he shouted, "I must let the king know how angry I am!"

Soon the town's smartest person came to the boulder in the road. She complained loudly that the king should do a better job of keeping the roads clear. Then she, too, walked around the boulder.

Finally, a farmer came along, carrying a load of vegetables. As soon as he arrived at the boulder, he set down his vegetables and tried to move the rock. "Other people might need to use this road," the farmer said to himself. "If I can move it, then I should do so."

After much hard work, the farmer finally succeeded in rolling the boulder off the road. He then noticed a hole where the boulder had been. Inside the hole was a box. The farmer opened the box to find the king's crown and a note. The note read, "For your hard work and for caring about others, you are now the king!"

1. What is one theme of the story?
- ○ Being rich is better than being wise.
- ● By taking time to help others, you may help yourself.
- ○ Farmers often make the best leaders.
- ○ Being rewarded makes a job less meaningful.

2. The wise king wanted the next king to be ___.
- ○ wealthy instead of poor
- ○ smart instead of rich
- ● a farmer instead of a merchant
- ○ a hard worker instead of a complainer

3. Which statement might the farmer most agree with?
- ○ Working hard has few rewards.
- ○ Complaining will get you noticed.
- ○ People should not concern themselves with things that are not their business.
- ● Helping others is rewarding.

4. What lesson did the wise king teach his subjects?
- ● More good comes from working hard than from complaining.
- ○ A king is not responsible for his subjects.
- ○ Everyone is equally important.
- ○ Always expect a difficult task to be rewarding.

Monday — WEEK 4 — 47

Page 48

Write It Right

Rewrite each sentence and correct the errors.

1. did you ride on won of the paddle boats along the missouri river
Did you ride on one of the paddle boats along the Missouri River?

2. larry shouted to one of his friend's at the game look at that
Larry shouted to one of his friends at the game, "Look at that!"

3. snails grasshoppers and other bugs nibbled on the plants in aunt mays garden
Snails, grasshoppers, and other bugs nibbled on the plants in Aunt May's garden.

MATH TIME

Use the rule listed at the top of each function table to help you complete the tables. The first ones have been done for you.

Rule: ×2 +3	
Input	Output
1	5
2	7
7	17
5	13
8	19
17	37

Rule: ×9 +3	
Input	Output
1	3
5	15
8	24
7	21
12	36
15	45

48 — Monday

Page 49

SPELL IT

There are several ways to spell words with the /er/ sound.
ir   er   ar   ear   or   ur

Fill in the letters that stand for the /er/ sound in the spelling words for the week.

1. p__ur__pose
2. p__ur__gent
3. th__ir__sty
4. c__er__tain
5. wond__er__
6. gramm__ar__
7. calend__ar__
8. __ear__th
9. __ear__ly
10. may__or__
11. smuggl__er__
12. p__ear__l

In My Own Words

What if you woke up one day on another planet? Write the beginning of a story, telling how you felt, what you saw, and the first thing you did.

Sample answer:
One morning I opened my eyes and almost fell out of bed. I couldn't believe what I saw! The whole world looked different. It was scary but also a little exciting. The grass was yellow, trees were orange, and the sky was purple. "Where am I?" I wondered. I decided to explore the area, even though I was still in my pajamas. Suddenly, I saw a very strange-looking animal. It was like a deer, but it was the size of an elephant, with huge antlers made out of tree branches. The deer looked at me and smiled. Then it said, "Good morning, Earthling!" That's when I knew I was on another planet.

Tuesday — WEEK 4 — 49

Answer Key

Page 50

LANGUAGE LINES

Pronouns are used in place of nouns. Examples of pronouns include he, she, and it.

Underline the pronoun in the second sentence of each pair. On the line, write the noun that the pronoun replaced.

1. The bus is coming. <u>It</u> is late. — bus
2. Mr. Jefferson is the driver. <u>He</u> is usually on time. — Mr. Jefferson
3. Isaiah and Felicia are laughing. <u>They</u> love a joke. — Isaiah and Felicia
4. Carmen is laughing. <u>She</u> is usually reading quietly. — Carmen
5. Tony sits next to Carlos. Tony is grinning at <u>him</u>. — Carlos
6. Carlos is looking at Rosa. Carlos is smiling at <u>her</u>. — Rosa
7. Why are the kids laughing? What happened to <u>them</u>? — the kids
8. My brother Ian and I want to know. What did <u>we</u> miss? — Ian and I
9. Tony looks at Ian and me. Then Tony tells <u>us</u>. — Ian and me
10. Tony, Ian, and I laugh. <u>We</u> laugh the whole way to school. — Tony, Ian, and I

MATH TIME

Solve the word problems about a camping trip taken by a group of Scouts.

1. During the camping trip, 9 Scouts can sleep in a cabin. All boys or all girls must sleep in each cabin. If there are 70 boys and 76 girls, how many cabins will be needed to house all of the Scouts?

Answer: 17 cabins

2. The camping trip costs $25.00 per Scout. If there are 146 Scouts going on the trip, how much money will the scouts need in all?

Answer: $3,650

3. The Scouts held a fundraiser to help pay for the trip. They raised $1,562. If they split the money between all 146 Scouts, how much will each Scout still owe for the trip? Round to the nearest dollar.

Answer: $14

Page 51

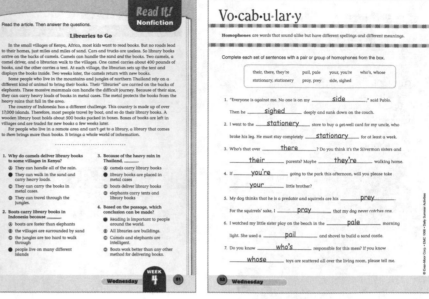

Read the article. Then answer the questions.

Libraries to Go

In the small villages of Kenya, Africa, most kids want to read books. But no roads lead to their homes, just miles and miles of sand. Cars and trucks are useless. So library books arrive on the backs of camels. Camels can handle the sand *and* the books. Two camels, a camel driver, and a librarian walk to the villages. One camel carries about 400 pounds of books, and the other carries a tent. At each village, the librarian sets up the tent and displays the books inside. Two weeks later, the camels return with new books.

The country of Indonesia has a different challenge. This country is made up of over 17,000 islands. Therefore, most people travel by boat, and so do their library books. A wooden library boat holds about 500 books packed in boxes. Boxes of books are left in villages and are traded for new books a few weeks later.

For people who live in a remote area and can't get to a library, a library that comes *to them* brings more than books. It brings a whole world of information.

1. Why do camels deliver library books to some villages in Kenya?
   - Ⓐ They can handle all of the rain.
   - ● They can walk in the sand and carry heavy loads.
   - Ⓒ They can carry the books in metal cases.
   - Ⓓ They can travel through the jungles.

2. Boats carry library books in Indonesia because
   - Ⓐ boats are faster than elephants
   - Ⓑ the villages are surrounded by sand
   - Ⓒ the jungles are too hard to walk through
   - ● people live on many different islands

3. Because of the heavy rain in Thailand,
   - Ⓐ camels carry library books
   - ● library books are placed in metal cases
   - Ⓒ boats deliver library books
   - Ⓓ elephants carry tents and library books

4. Based on the passage, which conclusion can be made?
   - ● Reading is important to people around the world.
   - Ⓑ All libraries are buildings.
   - Ⓒ Camels and elephants are intelligent.
   - Ⓓ Boats work better than any other method for delivering books.

Page 52

Vo·cab·u·lar·y

Homophones are words that sound alike but have different spellings and different meanings.

Complete each set of sentences with a pair or group of homophones from the box.

their, there, they're	pail, pale	your, you're	who's, whose
stationary, stationery	pray, prey	side, sighed	

1. "Everyone is against me. No one is on my _____side_____," said Pablo.
   Then he _____sighed_____ deeply and sunk down on the couch.

2. I went to the _____stationery_____ store to buy a get-well card for my uncle, who broke his leg. He must stay completely _____stationary_____ for at least a week.

3. Who's that over _____there_____? Do you think it's the Silverman sisters and _____their_____ parents? Maybe _____they're_____ walking home.

4. If _____you're_____ going to the park this afternoon, will you please take _____your_____ little brother?

5. My dog thinks that he is a predator and squirrels are his _____prey_____.
   For the squirrels' sake, I _____pray_____ that my dog never catches one.

6. I watched my little sister play on the beach in the _____pale_____ morning light. She used a _____pail_____ and shovel to build a sand castle.

7. Do you know _____who's_____ responsible for this mess? If you know _____whose_____ toys are scattered all over the living room, please tell me.

Page 53

LANGUAGE LINES

A verb must agree in number with its subject. If the subject is singular, the verb must be singular. If the subject is plural, the verb must be plural.

Read each sentence. If the subject-verb agreement is correct, write correct on the line. If the subject-verb agreement is not correct, rewrite the sentence correctly.

1. At the Aquarium, I learns about coral reefs.
   At the Aquarium, I learn about coral reefs.

2. Our guide teaches us about jellyfish.
   correct

3. Carla and Joe likes the shark tank.
   Carla and Joe like the shark tank.

4. We ask the guide a lot of questions.
   correct

In My Own Words

Imagine you found a $100 bill lying on the ground. What would you do with the money?

Sample answer:
I would take half of it and put it into a savings account. I would give the other half to an animal shelter, since that is my favorite charity.

Page 54

Mind Jigglers

Who Ate What?

The Jones family went out for dinner. Each person ordered something different. Read the clues and fill in the chart to find out what each person ordered. Make an X in a box when it *cannot* be an answer. Draw a circle in the box when it is the correct answer.

	Grandpa	Grandma	Dad	Mom	Josh	Becca
Hamburger	X	X	X	X	O	X
Lasagna	X	X	X	O	X	X
Fish and chips	X	O	X	X	X	X
Baked salmon	O	X	X	X	X	X
Spaghetti	X	X	X	X	X	O
Chicken strips	X	X	O	X	X	X

1. None of the males in the family ordered a dinner that contained pasta.

2. None of the adults ordered a hamburger.

3. The person who ordered spaghetti is younger than the person who ordered lasagna.

4. Dad is allergic to fish.

5. Grandma did not order lasagna.

6. The person who ordered salmon shared some of it with his wife.

Page 55

MATH TIME

Find the Volume

Jamal wants to buy the fish tank that will hold the most water. Determine the volume of each rectangular prism. Circle the tank with the greatest volume.

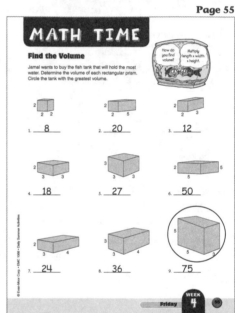

1. 8
2. 20
3. 12
4. 18
5. 27
6. 50
7. 24
8. 36
9. 75 (circled)

Page 56

Geography

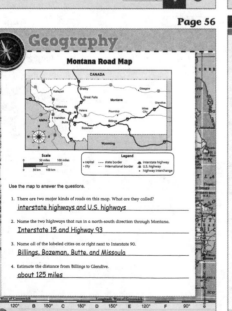

Montana Road Map

Use the map to answer the questions.

1. There are two major kinds of roads on this map. What are they called?
   interstate highways and U.S. highways

2. Name the two highways that run in a north-south direction through Montana.
   Interstate 15 and Highway 93

3. Name all of the labeled cities on right next to Interstate 90.
   Billings, Bozeman, Butte, and Missoula

4. Estimate the distance from Billings to Glendive.
   about 125 miles

Page 59

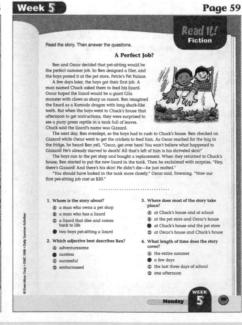

Read the story. Then answer the questions.

A Perfect Job?

Ben and Oscar decided that pet-sitting would be the perfect summer job. So Ben designed a flier, and the boys posted it at the pet store, Petrie's Pet Palace.

A few days later, the boys got their first job. A man named Chuck asked them to feed his lizard. Oscar hoped the lizard would be a giant Gila monster with claws as sharp as razors. Ben imagined the lizard as a Komodo dragon with long shark-like teeth. But when the boys went to Chuck's house that afternoon to get instructions, they were surprised to see a puny green reptile in a tank full of leaves. Chuck said the lizard's name was Gizzard.

The next day, Ben overslept, so the boys had to rush to Chuck's house. Ben checked on Gizzard while Oscar went to get the crickets to feed him. As Oscar reached for the bag in the fridge, he heard Ben yell, "Oscar, get over here! You won't believe what happened to Gizzard! He's already starved to death! All that's left of him is his shriveled skin!"

The boys ran to the pet shop and bought a replacement. When they returned to Chuck's house, Ben pointed to the new lizard in the tank. Then he exclaimed with surprise, "Hey, there's Gizzard! And there's his skin! He didn't die—he just molted."

"You should have looked in the tank more closely," Oscar said, frowning. "Now our first pet-sitting job cost us $20."

1. Whom is the story about?
   - Ⓐ a man who owns a pet shop
   - Ⓑ a man who has a lizard
   - Ⓒ a lizard that dies and comes back to life
   - ● two boys pet-sitting a lizard

2. Which adjective best describes Ben?
   - Ⓐ adventuresome
   - ● careless
   - Ⓒ successful
   - Ⓓ embarrassed

3. Where does most of the story take place?
   - Ⓐ at Chuck's house and at school
   - Ⓑ at the pet store and Oscar's house
   - ● at Chuck's house and the pet store
   - Ⓓ at Oscar's house and Chuck's house

4. What length of time does the story cover?
   - Ⓐ the entire summer
   - ● a few days
   - Ⓒ the last three days of school
   - Ⓓ one afternoon

Page 60

Write It Right

Rewrite each sentence and correct the errors.

1. can you come with my friends and i to central park
   Can you come with my friends and I to Central Park?

2. is adam spending august at lake mead or is he staying home
   Is Adam spending August at Lake Mead or is he staying home?

3. tammi shouted keep away from that broken bottle
   Tammi shouted, "Keep away from that broken bottle!"

4. me and tracie is going to the mall on soterday
   Tracie and I are going to the mall on Saturday.

MATH TIME

Complete the addition problems.

2.5	1.2	4.29	92.5	91.64
+ 6.4	+ 6.7	+ 4.31	+ 43.8	+ 15.28
8.9	7.9	8.60	136.3	106.92

24.90	15.300	12.5	51.6	21.951
+ 6.52	+ 5.915	+ 2.9	+ 4.0	+ 5.319
31.42	21.215	15.4	55.6	27.270

15.3	49.2	15.0	4.23	4.29
+ 84.6	+ 6.5	+ 6.4	+ 6.51	+ 93.34
99.9	55.7	21.4	10.74	97.63

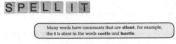

SPELL IT

Many words have consonants that are **silent**. For example,
the t is silent in the words **castle** and **hustle**.

Fill in the letters to complete the spelling words for the week. Then circle the silent consonant
or consonants in each word.

1. 〈wr〉e〈st〉le
2. an〈sw〉er
3. dou〈bt〉
4. 〈kn〉apsack
5. li〈st〉en
6. 〈is〉land
7. ta〈lk〉
8. desi〈gn〉
9. 〈kn〉owle〈dg〉e
10. nu〈mb〉
11. 〈h〉onor
12. wh〈istl〉e

In My Own Words

If you could have a superpower, which one would you choose?
How would you use your new power?

Sample answer:
I would choose flying. I would fly to see my family
in other states and to get to school every day. But I
would also try to use my flying to help other people,
such as by catching someone who was falling off a
tall building or by delivering important messages or
finding someone who was lost.

LANGUAGE LINES

An adjective describes a noun or a pronoun.

Underline the adjectives in the sentences.

1. Imagine going to a **big** cinema to see a **silent** movie.
2. You find a **comfortable** seat and watch the **large**, **dark** screen light up.
3. You expect the movie to be **exciting** and **entertaining**.
4. It stars a **handsome** actor and a **beautiful** actress, both of whom are **famous** celebrities.
5. But when they appear on the **huge** screen, you do not hear their voices.
6. **Silent** movies displayed words on the screen to tell stories that could be **funny** or **serious**.
7. The actors also exaggerated their **facial** expressions to show **dramatic** emotions.
8. You had to be a **good**, **fast** reader to watch a **silent** film.
9. Today, movies not only have sound but **amazing** effects.
10. These effects can make going to a movie a **memorable**—and **loud**—experience!

MATH TIME

Complete the subtraction problems.

61.2 − 60.1 **1.1**	5.9 − 2.3 **3.6**	4.1 − 3.9 **0.2**	12.9 − 9.2 **3.7**	15.9 − 7.8 **8.1**
12.1 − 5.8 **6.3**	15.26 − 5.49 **9.77**	4.59 − 2.00 **2.59**	83.49 − 2.95 **80.54**	8.00 − 5.12 **2.88**
51.2 − 14.1 **37.1**	96.0 − 5.8 **90.2**	49.2 − 15.9 **33.3**	91.0 − 2.5 **88.5**	16.29 − 5.49 **10.8**

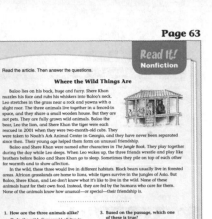

Read the article. Then answer the questions.

Read It! Nonfiction

Where the Wild Things Are

Baloo lies on his back, huge and furry. Shere Khan nuzzles his face and rubs his whiskers into Baloo's neck. Leo stretches in the grass near a rock and yawns with a slight roar. These animals live together in a fenced-in space, and they share a small wooden house. But they are not pets. They are fully grown wild animals. Baloo the bear, Leo the lion, and Shere Khan the tiger were each rescued in 2001 when they were two-month-old cubs. They were taken to Noah's Ark Animal Center in Georgia, and they have never been separated since then. Their young age helped them form an unusual friendship.

Baloo and Shere Khan were named after characters in *The Jungle Book*. They play together during the day while Leo sleeps. When Leo wakes up, the three friends wrestle and play like brothers before Baloo and Shere Khan go to sleep. Sometimes they pile on top of each other for warmth and to show affection.

In the wild, these three would live in different habitats. Black bears usually live in forested areas. African grasslands are home to lions, while tigers survive in the jungles of Asia. But Baloo, Shere Khan, and Leo don't know what it's like to live in the wild. None of these animals hunt for their own food. Instead, they are fed by the humans who care for them. None of the animals know how unusual—or special—their friendship is.

1. How are the three animals alike?
   - Ⓐ In the wild, they would all live in forests.
   - Ⓑ They are all named for characters in a book.
   - ● They were all rescued at the same time.
   - Ⓓ They are all active during the day.

2. Unlike Baloo and Shere Khan, Leo is___.
   - Ⓐ wild
   - Ⓑ a meat eater
   - ● more active at night
   - Ⓓ a vegetarian

3. Based on the passage, which one of these is true?
   - Ⓐ Different animals cannot live together.
   - Ⓑ Bears prefer lions to tigers.
   - Ⓒ Zoos are the best place for any animal.
   - ● Bears usually have a different home than lions do.

4. Which one is true about Baloo?
   - ● He is fed by people who care for him.
   - Ⓑ He is most active at night.
   - Ⓒ He prefers Shere Khan to Leo.
   - Ⓓ He prefers to sleep by himself.

Vo·cab·u·lar·y

A compound word is a word made up of two or more smaller words. You might see the same smaller word in many different compound words.

Write the compound word that best replaces the underlined words in each sentence. Use a dictionary to help you, if necessary.

| uphold | upbeat | update | uproar |
| upstream | backdrop | backtracked | backfired |

1. The news of the soccer team's victory put our school in a major state of noisy confusion. — **uproar**
2. Pablo's scheme to trick his friend ended up causing the opposite effect from the one he wanted. His friend tricked him, instead! — **backfired**
3. The play's first act took place in front of a forest scene painted at the back of the stage. — **backdrop**
4. Andrea writes mournful poems, but my poems are more cheerful and optimistic. — **upbeat**
5. One of the government's jobs is to protect and defend people's civil rights. — **uphold**
6. Arguing for a plan of an unpopular plan can be like swimming against the current. — **upstream**
7. Mom asked for an explanation of the latest details on my math grade. — **update**
8. When I noticed that I'd lost a mitten, I retraced my steps until I found it. — **backtracked**

LANGUAGE LINES

Negatives are words that mean "no" or "not."

Write the correct negative from the word box to complete each sentence.

| no | not | never | nowhere |

1. Shirenda **never** remembers her sister's birthday.
2. She has **no** idea why it's so hard to remember.
3. We **never** forget Shauna's birthday.
4. We know that Shauna will go **nowhere** on her birthday without Shirenda.
5. There is **no** way we're going to let Shirenda forget again.
6. This year, Shirenda does **not** stand a chance!
7. We'll **never** let her rest until she has bought a card and a present.
8. This is **not** going to be like any other year for Shauna.

In My Own Words

Have you ever had something weird or scary happen to you? Describe the event.

Sample answer:
One time I was sitting in my room alone when all
of a sudden, my door slammed shut and my light
went off! The weird thing is that my window was
closed, so there wasn't any wind, and there was no
storm that could cause a power outage. My dad says
that an open window across the hall blew the door
shut, and the slam caused a loose light bulb in my
lamp to flicker out. But I still think it was a ghost.

Mind Jigglers

Playful Plates

Some people have special license plates with letters and numbers that create a message. What do the plates below say? The first one has been done for you.

1. **IML8** — I'm late.
2. **LUV2SKI** — love to ski
3. **RUHAPE** — Are you happy?
4. **CR8TIV** — creative
5. **ICU2** — I see you, too.
6. **L8R G8R** — later gator
7. **1GR8GAL** — one great gal
8. **CRAZ4U** — crazy for you
9. **QT PIE** — cutie pie
10. **UR2SLO** — You are too slow.

MATH TIME

The Solar System

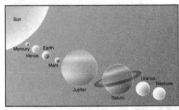

1. Mercury is about 58 million kilometers from the sun, and Earth is about 155 million kilometers from the sun. How much farther away from the sun is Earth than Mercury?

   97 million kilometers

2. The diameter of Earth is 12,756 kilometers, the diameter of Saturn is 120,600 kilometers, and the diameter of Uranus is 51,300 kilometers. Is the sum of these three planets more or less than Jupiter's diameter of 142,200 kilometers? How much more or less is it?

   42,456 kilometers more

3. A year on Jupiter is about 12 Earth years. If a year on Earth is 365 days, how many days would a year on Jupiter be?

   4,380 days

Geography

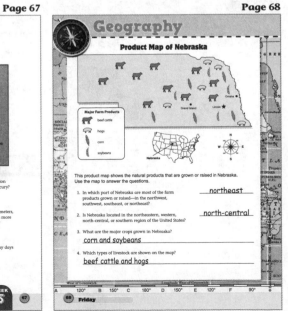

Product Map of Nebraska

Major Farm Products
- beef cattle
- hogs
- corn
- soybeans

This product map shows the natural products that are grown or raised in Nebraska. Use the map to answer the questions.

1. In which part of Nebraska are most of the farm products grown or raised—in the northwest, southwest, southeast, or northeast? — **northeast**
2. Is Nebraska located in the northeastern, western, north-central, or southern region of the United States? — **north-central**
3. What are the major crops grown in Nebraska? — **corn and soybeans**
4. Which types of livestock are shown on the map? — **beef cattle and hogs**

Read the article. Then answer the questions.

Read It! Nonfiction

Life on Jupiter's Icy Moon

Jupiter is the largest planet in our solar system and is made up of many different kinds of gases. It is so big that 1,300 Earths could fit *inside* Jupiter. It also has 63 moons. Some of its moons are like small planets, and others are pieces of frozen rock and ice. Studying Jupiter's moons has helped scientists learn more about the solar system. But the moon that scientists are most interested in is Europa (yur-OH-pa).

The conditions on Europa make it the most likely place in the solar system, besides Earth, to have life. It is covered in a layer of ice, and some scientists believe a liquid ocean lies beneath the icy surface. If this is true, Europa may have simple forms of life in these oceans. The creatures on Europa would probably be too small to see without a microscope. But the idea of anything at all living on Europa is very exciting.

Right now, we cannot explore Europa because it is too cold and too far away to send people there. The spacecrafts and robots we have are not sturdy enough to land on the surface. But scientists have big plans. In the future, they hope to send one robot to melt some of the ice on Europa's surface, and another robot to swim through its oceans. The information that these robots gather could change what we think about life beyond Earth.

1. What is the passage mostly about?
   - Ⓐ Jupiter's many moons
   - ● possible life on Europa
   - Ⓒ scientists' search for new life
   - Ⓓ the problem with exploring outer space

2. Which of these explains why scientists think life could exist on Europa?
   - Ⓐ The creatures would be too small to see without a microscope.
   - Ⓑ Europa is one of Jupiter's 63 moons.
   - ● Europa has a layer of ice that may have liquid below it.
   - Ⓓ Jupiter is the solar system's largest planet.

3. What is the main idea of the last paragraph?
   - ● Exploring Europa is very difficult.
   - Ⓑ People are better than robots.
   - Ⓒ Scientists want to discover new life.
   - Ⓓ Life can only be discovered by machines.

4. Europa is best described as___.
   - Ⓐ warm and full of life
   - Ⓑ cold and uninteresting
   - ● icy and mysterious
   - Ⓓ cool and dry

---

134 Answer Key

Page 72

Write It Right

Rewrite each sentence and correct the errors.

1. that greedy little child drinked all the cold lemonade they done had

   That greedy little child drank all the cold lemonade they had.

2. terrys brothers afraid of the dark so his mom gived him a flashlight

   Terry's brother is (or brother's) afraid of the dark, so his mom gave him a flashlight.

3. my mothers favorite poem by robert frost is the road not taken

   My mother's favorite poem by Robert Frost is "The Road Not Taken."

MATH TIME

Complete the multiplication problems.

1. 2.0 x 0.1 = **0.2**
2. 4.0 x 0.5 = **2**
3. 8.0 x 0.25 = **2**
4. 5.0 x 0.5 = **2.5**
5. 1.0 x 0.75 = **0.75**
6. 3.5 x 0.5 = **1.75**
7. 3.0 x 0.25 = **0.75**
8. 2.0 x 0.4 = **0.8**
9. 5.0 x 0.8 = **4**
10. 4.0 x 0.95 = **3.8**
11. 2.0 x 0.87 = **1.74**
12. 6.5 x 0.4 = **2.6**

72 Monday

Page 73

SPELL IT

The sound /f/ can be spelled several ways:
f ph gh ff

Fill in the blanks with the letter or letters that stand for the /f/ sound to make the spelling words for the week.

1. gra **ph**
2. ne **ph** ew
3. enou **gh**
4. **f** ourth
5. **ph** ysical
6. rou **gh** est
7. **ph** armacy
8. **f** ragile
9. brie **f** ly
10. trium **ph**
11. **f** ountain
12. sta **ff**

In My Own Words

Name a character from a book that you can identify with. Explain how you are similar to or different from that character.

Sample answer:
I can identify with Ron Weasely from the Harry Potter books because, like Ron, I come from a really large, happy family. Also, I am a loyal friend. So even though I am not a wizard, and I go to a regular school instead of Hogwarts School of Witchcraft and Wizardry, I can relate to a lot of what Ron goes through.

Tuesday **WEEK 6** **73**

Page 74

LANGUAGE LINES

A prepositional phrase is made up of a preposition, the object of the preposition, and any words in between. Some prepositional phrases describe verbs and adverbs.

Underline the prepositional phrase in each sentence. Draw an arrow from the prepositional phrase to the verb or adverb it describes. Then circle *when* or *where* to explain what the phrase tells. The first one has been done for you.

1. The rain falls from the sky. when (where)
2. I hear the water rushing down the windows. when (where)
3. The lightning crackles before each thunderbolt. (when) where
4. I creep deeper under my quilt. (when) where
5. The house shakes after each jolt as the storm rages. (when) where
6. The wind screams loudly through the trees outside. when (where)
7. I worry that the roof might blow off the house. when (where)
8. I wonder if a tornado is headed toward us! when (where)

MATH TIME

Solve the word problems about earning money.

1. Max walked dogs to earn money. He charged $16 per week to walk one dog for 30 minutes per day. He walked 21 dogs every week. How much money did he earn in four weeks?

   Answer: **$1,344**

2. Arturo mowed lawns to earn money. He mowed 14 lawns each week and charged $24 to mow each one. How much did he earn in 12 weeks?

   Answer: **$4,032**

3. Cathy and Chris sold homemade cookies for $6 a bag. The girls sold 180 bags. Half of the money they collected paid for the cookie ingredients. The other half was their profit. How much profit did the girls make?

   Answer: **$540**

74 Tuesday

Page 75

Read It!
Fiction

Read the story. Then answer the questions.

The Boy Who Cried "Pirates!"

Long ago, a boy named Johnny lived on a ship that sailed the seas. His father was the captain. Johnny continually begged his father to let him keep watch. "Life on the sea is dangerous," his father said. "Only the most responsible sailors can keep watch for sudden storms or fearsome pirates."

One night, after much complaining and begging, the captain allowed Johnny to keep watch. Johnny expected the work to be exciting, but time crept more slowly than a slug. So Johnny decided to have some fun.

"Pirates! Pirates!" Johnny yelled out. The sailors scrambled on deck, only to see Johnny laughing. "Just kidding!" he said as his eyes filled with tears of laughter.

The captain was furious. "Pirates are no joke," he scolded. He made Johnny promise to behave, but Johnny did not listen. Once again, when everyone was asleep, he sounded the alarm. Sleepy sailors hurried to their posts, ready for action. And again, Johnny laughed at the fun of tricking them.

The third time Johnny was on watch, he yawned and stretched, scanning the horizon. To his shock, he saw an actual pirate ship in the distance. "P-p-pirates!" he stammered. "PIRATES!" But the sailors merely rolled over in their hammocks. They were sure Johnny was lying again. As the pirate ship edged closer, Johnny's heart beat quickly with fear. He realized that there was nothing funny about this.

1. Why do you think Johnny claims to see a pirate ship when he does not?
   Ⓐ to disobey his father, the captain
   Ⓑ to prove he has better eyes than the sailors
   ● to trick the sailors
   Ⓓ to show that he is young but brave

2. Why does Johnny continue to lie?
   ● He likes fooling the others.
   Ⓑ The sailors do not seem to mind.
   Ⓒ He does not know he is lying.
   Ⓓ The captain tells him to lie.

3. How does Johnny change at the end?
   Ⓐ He was lazy but becomes hardworking.
   Ⓑ He was helpful but decides to be a pirate.
   ● He was foolish but realizes his mistakes.
   Ⓓ He was silly but becomes trustworthy.

4. What is a theme of the story?
   Ⓐ You should ask for help even if you do not need it.
   Ⓑ Standing watch on a ship is boring.
   Ⓒ You can trick people forever.
   ● Liars are not believed, even when they tell the truth.

Wednesday **WEEK 6** **75**

Page 76

Vo·cab·u·lar·y

Antonyms are words with opposite meanings. For example, **happy** is an antonym of **sad**.

A. Complete each sentence by writing an antonym from the box on the line above the word in parentheses.

villain	accept	public	certain
original	youthful	sensible	professional

1. Which is the most **sensible** solution to our problem?
   (foolish)

2. I've never seen the **original** of that famous painting.
   (copy)

3. The president's inauguration is a **public** ceremony.
   (private)

4. Uncle Dave plans to **accept** the job offer.
   (refuse)

5. Our dog is 14 years old, but she still acts **youthful**.
   (elderly)

6. Some **professional** athletes earn millions of dollars a year.
   (amateur)

7. I studied for the test all weekend, so I'm **certain** I will pass.
   (doubtful)

8. By the end of a fairy tale, the **villain** is usually caught.
   (hero)

B. Choose a pair of antonyms from one of the sentences in Activity A. Write a sentence using both words.

Sample answer: George was doubtful that his team would win, even though his coach seemed certain about it.

Wednesday

Page 77

LANGUAGE LINES

Clipped words are shortened forms of longer words.

In each sentence, replace the underlined word with the correct clipped word from the box.

vet	fan	tie	champ	flu	pop	mini	burger

1. George is a soccer fanatic. **fan**
2. Rachel always listens to the station that plays popular music. **pop**
3. My sister has a miniature refrigerator for her dorm room. **mini**
4. Mom ordered a hamburger and fries. **burger**
5. Dan is the state diving champion. **champ**
6. Have you gotten your influenza shot yet? **flu**
7. Dad hates having to wear a necktie every day to work. **tie**
8. Max's grandfather is an army veteran. **vet**

In My Own Words

Write a "how-to" paragraph explaining something you know how to make or do.

Sample answer:
You can make pasta by first filling a large pot about three-quarters of the way with water. Place the pot on a burner, and set the heat to high. Once the water becomes hot, add about 2 tablespoons of salt to the water. When the water reaches a boil, put a box of pasta into the water. Cook the pasta between 8 and 10 minutes, or until soft. Then turn the burner off and carefully pour the pasta into a strainer to drain the water. You can now add whatever sauce you like!

Thursday **WEEK 6** **77**

Page 78

Mind Jigglers
Extreme Sports

A. Do you like extreme sports? Draw a star next to the sports that you have already tried. Write D next to the sports that you **definitely** want to try. Write M next to the sports that you **might** want to try. Write N next to the sports that you would **not** want to try.

Sample answers:

☆ snowboarding
☆ skateboarding
D in-line skating
M mountain biking
M rock climbing
N parasailing
N sky diving
N bungee jumping

N hang gliding
☆ surfing
M playing paintball
M stunt driving
M white-water rafting
D windsurfing
☆ wakeboarding

B. Solve the brainteasers.

Jen goes to the skate park every other day. Terry goes to the skate park every third day. Carlos goes to the skate park only on Mondays and Tuesdays. Today is Monday, June 3, and all 3 kids are at the skate park. On what date will they all be at the skate park again?

Day: **Tuesday**
Date: **July 9**

Eleven kids are at the skate park. Some of the kids have in-line skates (4 wheels per skate), some of them have skateboards (4 wheels per board), and some of them have bikes (2 wheels). There are 62 wheels altogether. How many kids are using each kind of equipment?

Sample answer:
In-line skates: **5**
Skateboards: **5**
Bikes: **1**

78 Thursday

Page 79

MATH TIME

Units of Measurement

Use the information in the box to help you convert the measurements below.

Remember:
12 inches = 1 foot
3 feet = 1 yard
5,280 feet = 1 mile
1 centimeter = 10 millimeters
1 meter = 100 centimeters
1 kilometer = 1,000 meters

U.S. System

1. 24 inches = **2** feet
2. 1 mile = **5,280** feet
3. 3 yards = **9** feet
4. 5 feet = **60** inches
5. 15 feet = **5** yards
6. 3 miles = **5,280** yards
7. 6 feet = **72** inches
8. 1.5 miles = **7,920** feet
9. 48 inches = **4** feet
10. 12 yards = **36** feet
11. 4 yards = **144** inches
12. 72 inches = **2** yards

Metric System

1. 1 meter = **100** centimeters
2. 1 kilometer = **1,000** meters
3. ½ meter = **50** centimeters
4. 500 meters = **½** kilometer
5. 3 meters = **3,000** millimeters
6. 8,000 meters = **8** kilometers
7. 500 millimeters = **½** meter
8. 500 centimeters = **5** meters
9. 1.5 kilometers = **150,000** centimeters
10. 13 meters = **13,000** centimeters
11. 133 meters = **133,000** millimeters
12. ¼ kilometer = **250** meters

Friday **WEEK 6** **79**

Page 80

Geography

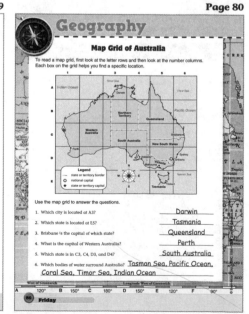

Map Grid of Australia

To read a map grid, first look at the letter rows and then look at the number columns. Each box on the grid helps you find a specific location.

Use the map grid to answer the questions.

1. Which city is located at A3? **Darwin**
2. Which state is located at E5? **Tasmania**
3. Brisbane is the capital of which state? **Queensland**
4. What is the capital of Western Australia? **Perth**
5. Which state is in C3, C4, D3, and D4? **South Australia**
6. Which bodies of water surround Australia? **Tasman Sea, Pacific Ocean, Coral Sea, Timor Sea, Indian Ocean**

80 Friday

Answer Key **135**

Week 7

Page 83

Read It! Nonfiction

Read the article. Then answer the questions.

A Patient Parent

Adults may tell you that it's tough being a parent. But they have it easy compared to the emperor penguin. This parent has one of the toughest jobs in the animal kingdom.

Emperor penguins mate in Antarctica in March or April. The female lays an egg in May or June. Then the mother penguin carefully passes the egg to the father, who balances it on top of his feet. The penguins must be very careful not to drop the egg, as it can crack or freeze if it touches the ground.

The mother leaves to find food, and the father waits patiently for the egg to hatch. This usually takes at least 60 days. During that time, the father doesn't eat, and he must stay very still so he doesn't hurt the egg.

By the time the chick hatches, the father is very weak. But he must feed the baby if the mother has not yet returned. He does this by making a special liquid in his throat. Luckily the mother penguin usually returns within a few days after the chick hatches. She feeds the chick and takes care of it so the father can go get food for himself. By this time, the male has gone 115 days without eating. Talk about a devoted dad!

1. **What does the mother penguin do right after she lays the egg?**
   - Ⓐ She finds food.
   - ● She gives the egg to the father.
   - Ⓒ She takes care of the egg.
   - Ⓓ She lets the father eat.
2. **What always happens before the chick hatches?**
   - Ⓐ The father leaves to find food.
   - Ⓑ The mother returns to care for the chick.
   - ● The father doesn't eat and barely moves.
   - Ⓓ The mother and father care for the chick together.
3. **Which of these does *not* happen after the chick hatches?**
   - Ⓐ The mother feeds the chick.
   - Ⓑ The mother returns with food.
   - ● The father leaves to find food.
   - Ⓓ The father sits without eating or moving.
4. **What is the last thing that happens after emperor penguins mate?**
   - Ⓐ The chick hatches from its egg.
   - Ⓑ The parents take turns caring for the chick.
   - ● The father leaves to eat.
   - Ⓓ The mother lays a new egg.

Monday WEEK 7 83

Page 84

Write It Right

Rewrite each sentence and correct the errors.

1. my brother and me need to bye shirts pants socks and shoes for school
   My brother and I need to buy shirts, pants, socks, and shoes for school.
2. when will the technician ms rawlings fix ours computer
   When will the technician, Ms. Rawlings, fix our computer?
3. they all singed happy birthday before her cut the cake
   They all sang "Happy Birthday" before she cut the cake.
4. we ain't got no fancy clothes for graduashun tomorrow
   We don't have any (*or* We have no *or* We've got no) fancy clothes for graduation tomorrow.

MATH TIME

Solve the multiplication problems.

$\frac{3}{4} \times \frac{1}{2} = \frac{3}{8}$	$\frac{5}{6} \times \frac{5}{7} = \frac{25}{42}$	$\frac{1}{8} \times \frac{3}{8} = \frac{3}{64}$
$\frac{2}{5} \times \frac{1}{3} = \frac{2}{15}$	$\frac{1}{5} \times \frac{2}{3} = \frac{2}{15}$	$\frac{5}{8} \times \frac{3}{7} = \frac{15}{56}$
$\frac{4}{7} \times \frac{1}{3} = \frac{4}{21}$	$\frac{4}{7} \times \frac{1}{9} = \frac{4}{63}$	$\frac{1}{2} \times \frac{5}{9} = \frac{5}{18}$
$\frac{2}{5} \times \frac{4}{5} = \frac{8}{25}$	$\frac{5}{9} \times \frac{4}{7} = \frac{20}{63}$	$\frac{2}{5} \times \frac{3}{7} = \frac{6}{35}$
$\frac{1}{2} \times \frac{1}{6} = \frac{1}{12}$	$\frac{1}{3} \times \frac{2}{7} = \frac{2}{21}$	$\frac{7}{9} \times \frac{10}{11} = \frac{70}{99}$
$\frac{3}{4} \times \frac{1}{5} = \frac{3}{20}$	$\frac{7}{8} \times \frac{3}{5} = \frac{21}{40}$	$\frac{1}{3} \times \frac{10}{13} = \frac{10}{39}$

84 Monday

Page 85

SPELL IT

Words that are often misspelled are called **spelling demons**.

Circle the correct spelling of each spelling demon.

1. (separate) seperate
2. travelor (traveler)
3. embarass (embarrass)
4. (occasion) ocassion
5. allready (already)
6. coff (cough)
7. busness (business)
8. (attendance) attendence
9. (discipline) disipline
10. rhythym (rhythm)
11. (appreciate) apreciate
12. sincerly (sincerely)

In My Own Words

In the story *Alice in Wonderland*, Alice fell down a rabbit hole and had many adventures. Imagine that you fell down a hole into a different world. Describe an adventure you might have.

Sample answer:
After falling down the hole, I landed in a world that was just like a video game. A screen came up and asked me which car I wanted. I picked a bright green convertible. Suddenly, I was in the car on a racetrack with other cars. I heard a countdown, and then we were off! I drove around a difficult course and bumped into other cars. Sometimes I even went off the road, but I was always in the lead. After three times around the course, I was declared the winner!

Tuesday WEEK 7 85

Page 86

LANGUAGE LINES

A sentence must express a complete thought. A group of words that does not express a complete thought is called a fragment.

Write *sentence* if the group of words expresses a complete thought and *fragment* if it does not.

1. The volcanoes of New Zealand. — fragment
2. Volcanoes formed New Zealand. — sentence
3. The ash and lava created interesting landforms. — sentence
4. With active volcanoes nearby. — fragment
5. New Zealanders live near active volcanoes. — sentence
6. Live on ranches in New Zealand. — fragment
7. Millions of sheep live on ranches. — sentence
8. Rugby, a kind of football. — fragment
9. New Zealanders love to play rugby. — sentence

MATH TIME

Solve the word problems.

1. Danny has 48 baseball cards in his collection. He would like to give $\frac{3}{4}$ of them to his little brother. How many should he give his brother?
   Answer: 36 cards
2. Mary Anne has 60 troll dolls in her bedroom. Her parents have asked her to put $\frac{2}{3}$ of them away in storage because her room is too messy. How many does she need to put into storage?
   Answer: 40 dolls
3. Miguel is collecting stamps. He has 120 pages in his stamp book. If $\frac{3}{5}$ of the pages are filled with stamps, how many blank pages are there in Miguel's book?
   Answer: 48 blank pages
4. Brendan has a rock collection that weighs 200 pounds. His dad tried to lift it and realized it was too heavy. He was only able to lift $\frac{5}{8}$ of the collection at once. How many pounds of rocks was Brendan's dad able to lift?
   Answer: 125 lbs

86 Tuesday

Page 87

Read It! Fiction

Read the story. Then answer the questions.

Mighty Stormalong

Have you heard of Stormalong, the tallest, biggest sailor there ever was? When Stormalong was born, he was so big that he was given a tree branch for a rattle. When Stormalong was one year old, his mom and dad took the roof off the house so he wouldn't hit his head on it. Stormalong was taller than most buildings by the time he was two.

Stormalong's mom spent four years knitting a hammock for him to sleep in. It stretched from New Jersey to New York. Stormalong watched the ships sail up and down the Hudson River as he swayed in his bed.

When Stormalong turned 10 years old, he joined the crew of the *Humongous*. It was the biggest ship he could find. All went well as long as he stayed in the middle of the ship. But if he leaned to the side just a bit, the ship would lean, too, and the crew would tumble out.

Stormalong outgrew the *Humongous* when he was 13. So he built his own ship, the *Gigantic*. It was as fast as it was large. Stormalong decided to sail around the world. He left New York on a sunny day after a large breakfast of sausages as big as canoes. By the time he reached Florida, Stormalong was fast asleep. The *Gigantic* drifted south to Panama, the country that connects North America to South America. That ship was so big and heavy that it pushed right through the land and made the Panama Canal! Stormalong had created a shortcut between North and South America.

1. **Why did the author write the story?**
   - Ⓐ to tell the life story of a famous sailor
   - Ⓑ to persuade readers to write tales
   - Ⓒ to explain how a canal was actually built
   - ● to entertain readers with a silly tale about a giant
2. **Most of the author's descriptions of Stormalong are ______.**
   - ● exaggerations
   - Ⓑ historical facts
   - Ⓒ comparisons
   - Ⓓ opinions
3. **This story would most likely be found in a book ______.**
   - Ⓐ about the history of the Panama Canal
   - Ⓑ about famous sailing ships
   - ● of stories about imaginary people
   - Ⓓ about famous Americans
4. **The purpose of the last paragraph is to ______.**
   - ● tell a made-up version of how a famous landmark was formed
   - Ⓑ persuade people not to travel by ship
   - Ⓒ make tall people feel proud
   - Ⓓ describe an important sailing trip

Wednesday WEEK 7 87

Page 88

Vo•cab•u•lar•y

Homographs are words that sound the same and are spelled the same but have different meanings. For example, the word **hatch** is a homograph. It can mean "a small opening with a door" or "to come out."

Raise the hatch to climb into the attic. **Snakes hatch from eggs.**

Next to each sentence, write the letter that gives the meaning of the underlined homograph.

1. e — Put your dirty jeans in the hamper.
2. j — All of this rain will hamper the builders' progress.
3. k — Horses like to graze in the meadow.
4. b — Be careful not to graze your arm against the rough wooden fence.
5. n — Does your dog bay at the full moon?
6. d — There's a house on the cliff overlooking the bay.
7. i — The newborn lamb lies asleep in the stall.
8. m — This rainy weather might stall our plans to go fishing.
9. c — It is rare for me to have a soft drink.
10. g — The meat was too rare, so I cooked it longer.
11. h — I try to refrain from eating a lot of sugar.
12. f — The refrain is my favorite part of the song.
13. l — Be sure to lock the stable door.
14. a — I will keep the ladder stable as you climb.

a. firm, not shaky
b. to scrape
c. unusual; not often
d. a body of water near the coast
e. a basket for holding clothes
f. the chorus
g. cooked only for a short time
h. to hold oneself back from doing something
i. a pen inside a barn or stable
j. to disrupt or impede
k. to feed on growing grass
l. a building where animals are kept
m. to delay or prevent
n. to let out a long, howling bark

88 Wednesday

Page 89

LANGUAGE LINES

The subject tells who or what the sentence is about.
The predicate tells what the subject is or does.

Write the complete subject and predicate of each sentence. The first one has been done for you.

1. The excited shoppers rush into the department store.
   Subject: The excited shoppers — Predicate: rush into the department store
2. This denim jacket is on sale!
   Subject: This denim jacket — Predicate: is on sale
3. We will eat lunch in a restaurant.
   Subject: We — Predicate: will eat lunch in a restaurant
4. This juicy hamburger with pickles tastes good.
   Subject: This juicy hamburger with pickles — Predicate: tastes good

In My Own Words

Make a list of your five favorite foods. Explain why you like each one.

Sample answer:
1. hot dogs, because they are salty and juicy
2. pizza, because I like the gooey cheese
3. tacos, because I like spicy food
4. chocolate chip cookies, because they are sweet
5. pancakes, because they are warm and fluffy

Thursday WEEK 7 89

Page 90

Mind Jigglers

Look at each grid with a shaded design. Then imagine how the design would look if the grid was turned 90 degrees to the right. Shade the squares in the second grid to show how the design would look. The first one has been done for you.

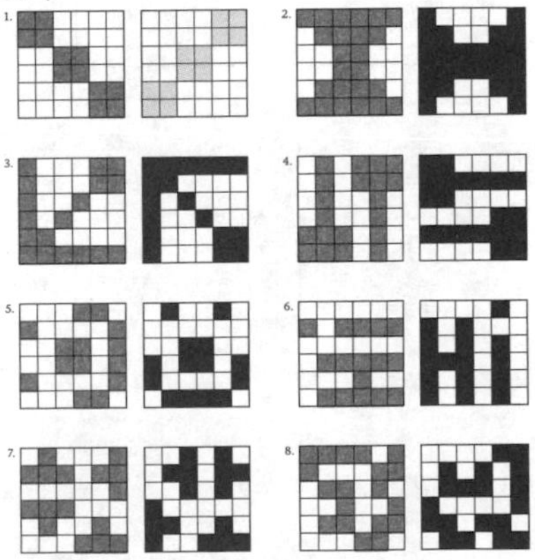

90 Thursday

Page 91

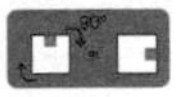

MATH TIME

Sports Stats

This table represents the different sports that boys and girls played at sports camp. Use the table to complete the double bar graph below for each sport.

	Football	Basketball	Soccer	Baseball	Golf
Boys	8	12	5	10	2
Girls	6	9	11	7	5

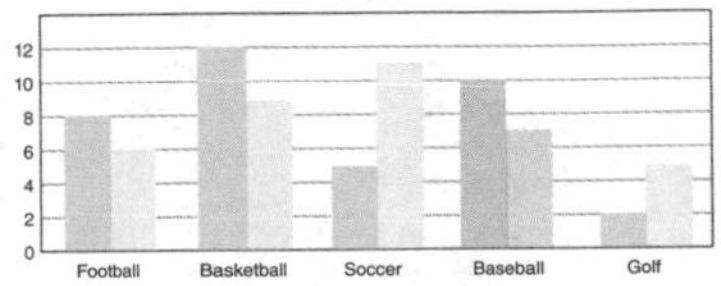

Use the table and graph to help you answer these questions.

1. How many more boys played basketball than girls? — three
2. Which sport did the most campers play? — basketball
3. Which sport did the fewest campers play? — golf
4. Which sport did the girls play most? — soccer
5. Did more boys or girls attend sports camp? How many more? — girls—one more

Friday WEEK 7 91

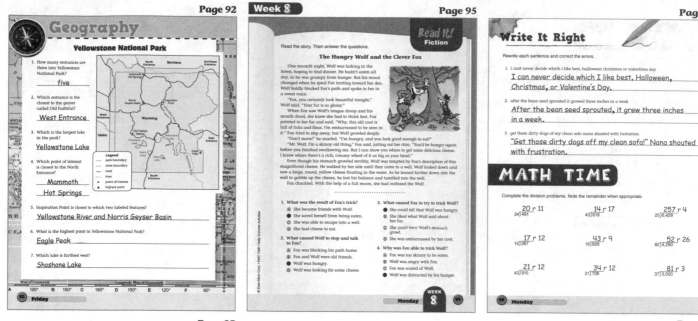

Page 92 — Geography

Yellowstone National Park

1. How many entrances are there into Yellowstone National Park?
   five

2. Which entrance is the closest to the geyser called Old Faithful?
   West Entrance

3. Which is the largest lake in the park?
   Yellowstone Lake

4. Which point of interest is closest to the North Entrance?
   Mammoth Hot Springs

5. Inspiration Point is closest to which two labeled features?
   Yellowstone River and Norris Geyser Basin

6. What is the highest point in Yellowstone National Park?
   Eagle Peak

7. Which lake is farthest west?
   Shoshone Lake

Friday

Page 95 — Read It! Fiction

Read the story. Then answer the questions.

The Hungry Wolf and the Clever Fox

One moonlit night, Wolf was lurking in the forest, hoping to find dinner. He hadn't eaten all day, so he was grumpy from hunger. But his mood changed when he spied Fox trotting toward her den. Wolf boldly blocked Fox's path and spoke to her in a sweet voice.

"Fox, you certainly look beautiful tonight," Wolf said. "Your fur is so glossy."

When Fox saw Wolf's tongue droop and his mouth drool, she knew she had to think fast. Fox pointed to her fur and said, "Why, this old coat is full of ticks and fleas. I'm embarrassed to be seen in it." Fox tried to step away, but Wolf growled deeply.

"Don't move!" he snarled. "I'm hungry, and you look good enough to eat!"

"Mr. Wolf, I'm a skinny old thing," Fox said, jutting out her chin. "You'd be hungry again before you finished swallowing me. But I can show you where to get some delicious cheese."

Even though his stomach growled terribly, Wolf was tempted by Fox's description of this magnificent cheese. He walked by her side until they came to a well. Wolf looked down and saw a large, round, yellow cheese floating in the water. As he leaned farther down into the well to gobble up the cheese, he lost his balance and tumbled into the well.

Fox chuckled. With the help of a full moon, she had outfoxed the Wolf.

1. What was the result of Fox's trick?
   Ⓐ She became friends with Wolf.
   ● She saved herself from being eaten.
   Ⓒ She was able to escape into a well.
   Ⓓ She had cheese to eat.

2. What caused Wolf to stop and talk to Fox?
   Ⓐ Fox was blocking his path home.
   Ⓑ Fox and Wolf were old friends.
   ● Wolf was hungry.
   Ⓓ Wolf was looking for some cheese.

3. What caused Fox to try to trick Wolf?
   Ⓐ She could tell that Wolf was hungry.
   Ⓑ She liked what Wolf said about her fur.
   Ⓒ She could hear Wolf's stomach growl.
   Ⓓ She was embarrassed by her coat.

4. Why was Fox able to trick Wolf?
   Ⓐ Fox was too skinny to be eaten.
   Ⓑ Wolf was angry with Fox.
   Ⓒ Fox was scared of Wolf.
   ● Wolf was distracted by his hunger.

Monday   Week 8

Page 96 — Write It Right

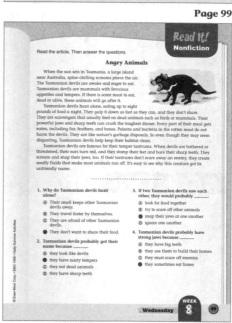

Rewrite each sentence and correct the errors.

1. i cant never decide which i like best, halloween christmas or valentines day
   I can never decide which I like best, Halloween, Christmas, or Valentine's Day.

2. after the bean seed sprouted it growed three inches in a week
   After the bean seed sprouted, it grew three inches in a week.

3. get them dirty dogs off my clean sofa nana shouted with frustration
   "Get those dirty dogs off my clean sofa!" Nana shouted with frustration.

MATH TIME

Complete the division problems. Note the remainder when appropriate.

$$24)\overline{491} = 20 \text{ r } 11$$
$$43)\overline{619} = 14 \text{ r } 17$$
$$25)\overline{6,429} = 257 \text{ r } 4$$

$$15)\overline{267} = 17 \text{ r } 12$$
$$19)\overline{826} = 43 \text{ r } 9$$
$$82)\overline{4,290} = 52 \text{ r } 26$$

$$43)\overline{915} = 21 \text{ r } 12$$
$$21)\overline{726} = 34 \text{ r } 12$$
$$37)\overline{3,000} = 81 \text{ r } 3$$

Monday

Page 97 — SPELL IT

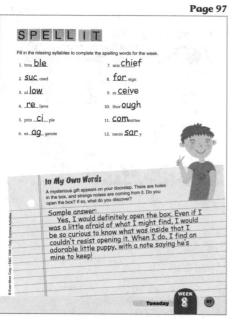

Fill in the missing syllables to complete the spelling words for the week.

1. trou **ble**
2. **suc** ceed
3. al **low**
4. **re** lieve
5. prin **ci** ple
6. ex **ag** gerate
7. mis **chief**
8. **for** eign
9. re **ceive**
10. thor **ough**
11. **com** mittee
12. neces **sar** y

In My Own Words

A mysterious gift appears on your doorstep. There are holes in the box, and strange noises are coming from it. Do you open the box? If so, what do you discover?

Sample answer:
Yes, I would definitely open the box. Even if I was a little afraid of what I might find, I would be so curious to know what was inside that I couldn't resist opening it. When I do, I find an adorable little puppy, with a note saying he's mine to keep!

Tuesday   Week 8

Page 98 — LANGUAGE LINES

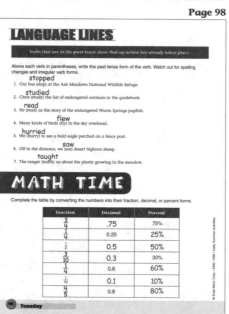

Verbs that are in the past tense show that an action has already taken place.

Above each verb in parentheses, write the past tense form of the verb. Watch out for spelling changes and irregular verb forms.

1. Our bus (stop) **stopped** at the Ash Meadows National Wildlife Refuge.
2. Chris (study) **studied** the list of endangered animals in the guidebook.
3. He (read) **read** us the story of the endangered Warm Springs pupfish.
4. Many kinds of birds (fly) **flew** in the sky overhead.
5. We (hurry) **hurried** to see a bald eagle perched on a fence post.
6. Off in the distance, we (see) **saw** desert bighorn sheep.
7. The ranger (teach) **taught** us about the plants growing in the meadow.

MATH TIME

Complete the table by converting the numbers into their fraction, decimal, or percent forms.

Fraction	Decimal	Percent
$\frac{3}{4}$	.75	75%
$\frac{1}{4}$	0.25	25%
$\frac{1}{2}$	0.5	50%
$\frac{3}{10}$	0.3	30%
$\frac{6}{10}$	0.6	60%
$\frac{1}{10}$	0.1	10%
$\frac{4}{5}$	0.8	80%

Tuesday

Page 99 — Read It! Nonfiction

Read the article. Then answer the questions.

Angry Animals

When the sun sets in Tasmania, a large island near Australia, spine-chilling screams pierce the air. The Tasmanian devils are awake and eager to eat. Tasmanian devils are mammals with ferocious appetites and tempers. If there is some meat to eat, dead or alive, these animals will go after it.

Tasmanian devils hunt alone, eating up to eight pounds of food a night. They gulp it down as fast as they can, and they don't share. They are scavengers that usually feed on dead animals such as birds or mammals. Their powerful jaws and sharp teeth can crush the toughest dinner. Every part of their meal gets eaten, including fur, feathers, and bones. Poisons and bacteria in the rotten meat do not harm the devils. They are like nature's garbage disposals. So even though they may seem disgusting, Tasmanian devils help keep their habitat clean.

Tasmanian devils are famous for their temper tantrums. When devils are bothered or threatened, their ears turn red, and they stomp their feet and bare their sharp teeth. They scream and snap their jaws, too. If their tantrums don't scare away an enemy, they create smelly fluids that make most animals run off. It's easy to see why this creature got its unfriendly name.

1. Why do Tasmanian devils hunt alone?
   Ⓐ Their smell keeps other Tasmanian devils away.
   Ⓑ They travel faster by themselves.
   Ⓒ They are afraid of other Tasmanian devils.
   ● They don't want to share their food.

2. Tasmanian devils probably got their name because _____
   ● they look like devils
   Ⓑ they have nasty tempers
   Ⓒ they eat dead animals
   Ⓓ they have sharp teeth

3. If two Tasmanian devils saw each other, they would probably _____
   Ⓐ look for food together
   Ⓑ try to scare off other animals
   ● snap their jaws at one another
   Ⓓ ignore one another

4. Tasmanian devils probably have strong jaws because _____
   Ⓐ they have big teeth
   Ⓑ they use them to build their homes
   Ⓒ they must scare off enemies
   ● they sometimes eat bones

Wednesday   Week 8

Page 100 — Vocabulary

A prefix is a word part that comes before a base word, root word, or other word part. A prefix changes a word's meaning.

The prefix inter– means "between" or "among."
The prefix trans– means "across."
The prefix circum– means "round" or "around."

Add the correct prefix from above to the beginning of each word part. Then write a sentence using the new word.

Sample sentences:

1. **trans** continental = "across a continent"
   My parents took a transcontinental flight to China.

2. **circum** navigate = "to go entirely around something"
   When I mow the lawn, I have to circumnavigate a large tree.

3. **circum** stances = "the situations surrounding an event"
   Despite the circumstances, Stacy was glad to see her family.

4. **inter** national = "between nations"
   The world leaders met at an international conference.

5. **trans** portation = "something that takes you across land or sea"
   After his car crash, Tom found another mode of transportation.

6. **inter** val = "the period of time between two events"
   The carpenter had a two-week interval between jobs.

7. **circum** ference = "the outer boundary of a circular area"
   The circumference of a beach ball is larger than that of a soccer ball.

Wednesday

Page 101 — LANGUAGE LINES

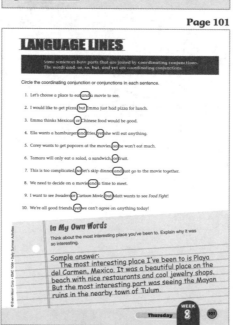

Some sentences have parts that are joined by coordinating conjunctions. The words and, or, so, but, and yet are coordinating conjunctions.

Circle the coordinating conjunction or conjunctions in each sentence.

1. Let's choose a place to eat (and) a movie to see.
2. I would like to get pizza (but) Emma just had pizza for lunch.
3. Emma thinks Mexican (or) Chinese food would be good.
4. Ella wants a hamburger (and) fries, (yet) she will eat anything.
5. Corey wants to get popcorn at the movies (so) he won't eat much.
6. Tamara will only eat a salad, a sandwich (or) fruit.
7. This is too complicated, (so) let's skip dinner (and) just go to the movie together.
8. We need to decide on a movie (and) a time to meet.
9. I want to see Invaders (or) Cartoon Movie (but) Matt wants to see Food Fight!
10. We're all good friends, (yet) we can't agree on anything today!

In My Own Words

Think about the most interesting place you've been to. Explain why it was so interesting.

Sample answer:
The most interesting place I've been to is Playa del Carmen, Mexico. It was a beautiful place on the beach with nice restaurants and cool jewelry shops. But the most interesting part was seeing the Mayan ruins in the nearby town of Tulum.

Thursday   Week 8

Page 102 — Mind Jigglers

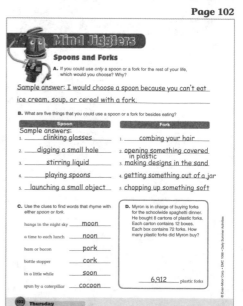

Spoons and Forks

A. If you could use only a spoon or a fork for the rest of your life, which would you choose? Why?

Sample answer: I would choose a spoon because you can't eat ice cream, soup, or cereal with a fork.

B. What are five things that you could use a spoon or a fork for besides eating?

Sample answers:

Spoon	Fork
1. clinking glasses	1. combing your hair
2. digging a small hole	2. opening something covered in plastic
3. stirring liquid	3. making designs in the sand
4. playing spoons	4. getting something out of a jar
5. launching a small object	5. chopping up something soft

C. Use the clues to find words that rhyme with either spoon or fork.

hangs in the night sky — **moon**
a time to each lunch — **noon**
ham or bacon — **pork**
bottle stopper — **cork**
in a little while — **soon**
spun by a caterpillar — **cocoon**

D. Myron is in charge of buying forks for the schoolwide spaghetti dinner. He bought 8 cartons of plastic forks. Each carton contains 12 boxes. Each box contains 72 forks. How many plastic forks did Myron buy?

6,912 plastic forks

Thursday

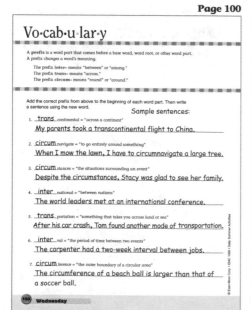

MATH TIME

Draw each line segment listed below, using a ruler or a straight edge. Then complete the sentence.

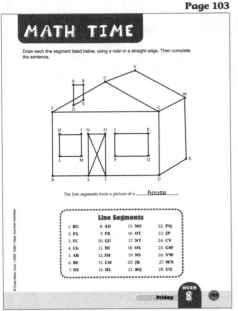

The line segments form a picture of a __house__

Line Segments

1. RU	8. AD	15. NO	22. PQ
2. FG	9. FR	16. OT	23. JP
3. FC	10. GU	17. NT	24. CV
4. CG	11. HI	18. OS	25. GW
5. AB	12. IM	19. NS	26. VW
6. BE	13. LM	20. JK	27. WX
7. DE	14. HL	21. KQ	28. UX

Geography

The Saint Lawrence Seaway

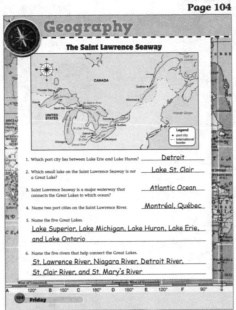

1. Which port city lies between Lake Erie and Lake Huron? __Detroit__

2. Which small lake on the Saint Lawrence Seaway is not a Great Lake? __Lake St. Clair__

3. Saint Lawrence Seaway is a major waterway that connects the Great Lakes to which ocean? __Atlantic Ocean__

4. Name two port cities on the Saint Lawrence River. __Montréal, Québec__

5. Name the five Great Lakes. __Lake Superior, Lake Michigan, Lake Huron, Lake Erie, and Lake Ontario__

6. Name the five rivers that help connect the Great Lakes. __St. Lawrence River, Niagara River, Detroit River, St. Clair River, and St. Mary's River__

Read It! Nonfiction

Read the article. Then answer the questions.

Destruction and Recovery

The eruption of Mount St. Helens, a volcano in southwestern Washington, was the most destructive eruption in North America ever recorded. It happened on May 18, 1980. Inside the volcano, hot melted rock, or magma, had been rising toward the surface for weeks. This rock was under intense pressure. On the day of the eruption, an earthquake caused the north side of the mountain peak to collapse and slide into the valley. Without the weight of the mountaintop, the pressure inside the volcano was released. As a result, a huge explosion sent steam, dust, rock, and ash soaring into the sky.

In a matter of minutes, the landslide and explosion completely destroyed an area 12 miles long by 18 miles wide. Thousands of towering old trees were flattened and buried in hot dust, ash, and rock. Fifty-seven people were killed. Hundreds of homes and miles of highway were destroyed. No large animals close to the blast survived. The only creatures that lived through the blast were those hidden in underground burrows.

Today, life is almost back to normal on Mount St. Helens. Even the areas that were most badly scorched and buried are now blanketed with wildflowers. Deer and elk are thriving. And millions of trees that people planted after the 1980 eruption are already growing tall. Scientists predict that in 200 years, if the volcano has not erupted again, the area will have completely returned to the way it was.

1. Why do you think the animals that lived underground were the only ones to survive the eruption?
   - ● They were protected from the falling ash and rock.
   - Ⓑ They were smarter than the other animals.
   - Ⓒ They had prepared for the eruption.
   - Ⓓ They lived farther away from the volcano.

2. How do you think scientists know it will take 200 years for Mount St. Helens to recover completely?
   - ● They know how long plants take to grow.
   - Ⓑ They know how long the recovery took last time.
   - Ⓒ The people who live there told them.
   - Ⓓ They can tell from the way the animals act.

3. What caused Mount St. Helens to finally erupt?
   - Ⓐ Intense pressure suddenly melted the rock.
   - Ⓑ The magma became very hot.
   - Ⓒ Dust, ash, and rock pushed the magma out.
   - ● An earthquake collapsed the mountain peak.

4. Why do you think deer are thriving on Mount St. Helens today?
   - ● because they survived the eruption
   - Ⓑ because they can live underground
   - Ⓒ because they have food to eat now
   - Ⓓ because all the animals that eat them died

Write It Right

Rewrite each sentence and correct the errors.

1. the reporter askd do u plan to run for re-election mr president
   __The reporter asked, "Do you plan to run for re-election, Mr. President?"__

2. the house shaked dishes rattled and the dog howled it was a earthquake
   __The house shook, dishes rattled, and the dog howled. It was an earthquake!__

3. rita bought her favorite book island of the blue dolphins on sale
   __Rita bought her favorite book, Island of the Blue Dolphins, on sale.__

MATH TIME

Complete the addition problems.

25 + 91 = 116	827 + 51 = 878	841 + 259 = 1,100	1,353 + 549 = 1,902
229 + 77 = 306	420 + 38 = 458	761 + 219 = 980	4,022 + 785 = 4,807
372 + 28 = 400	42 + 96 = 138	915 + 222 = 1,137	2,134 + 1,966 = 4,100

SPELL IT

Use these Greek and Latin word parts to help you make spelling words that fit each meaning.

bio = life · geo = earth · cycle = circle · auto = self · logy = study of · bi = two
port = carry · act = do · photo = light · trans = across · graph = write

1. the study of the earth __geology__
2. a story you write about your own life __autobiography__
3. to carry something across a distance __transport__
4. to record using light __photograph__
5. something that you do or complete __action__
6. the study of living things __biology__
7. self-acting __automatic__
8. able to be easily carried __portable__
9. a vehicle with two wheels __bicycle__
10. a rotating storm __cyclone__
11. a written account of someone else's life __biography__
12. to carry out or put into action __enact__

In My Own Words

Suppose you woke up one morning and were as small as a mouse. What are some advantages of your new size? What are some disadvantages?

Sample answer:
   I could get into very small spaces easily. I could overhear what people say without them knowing. But if I am spotted, people might be scared and try to trap me. Also, other animals might eat me!

LANGUAGE LINES

Independent clauses can stand alone as complete sentences.
Dependent clauses cannot stand alone.

Read each clause. Circle independent or dependent.

1. while we were sleeping one night — independent / (dependent)
2. a thunderstorm blew in from the north — (independent) / dependent
3. rain pelted the windows of my bedroom — (independent) / dependent
4. although I'm a sound sleeper — independent / (dependent)
5. I awoke with a start — (independent) / dependent
6. when I heard the first clap of thunder — independent / (dependent)
7. since I had left the window open — independent / (dependent)
8. my books on the windowsill are wet — (independent) / dependent

MATH TIME

Write true or false next to each math sentence.

< means less than	> means greater than
≤ means less than or equal to	≥ means greater than or equal to

1. 6.2 < 6.21 __true__
2. 4.5 ≤ 4.51 __true__
3. 4.2 > 4.4 __false__
4. 2.1 ≥ 2.5 __false__
5. 5.3 > 4.98 __true__
6. 2.3 ≤ 2.30 __true__
7. 2.1 < 2.18 __true__
8. 4.0 > 4 __false__
9. 4.2 ≥ 4.18 __true__
10. 5.1 > 5.6 __false__

Read It! Fiction

Read the story. Then answer the questions.

Checking Out Giants

"Come on, Jesse! Let's find ourselves some giants!" yelled Max.

"Everything is giant here," said Jesse softly. "This place is huge." Oak and cypress trees greeted the boys as they started on a trail through the state park. The shady path was just wide enough for the two cousins to walk side by side.

Jesse enjoyed the peace and quiet after two hours of being in the car with Max. The only sound he heard was the occasional twitter of birds—until Max started complaining.

"We should have watched the Giants' baseball game instead of looking for a bunch of stupid, giant trees," Max said. Jesse ignored him and focused on the cool breeze and the smell of damp soil.

"Got any water, Jesse?" Max asked loudly, making Jesse jump. Jesse handed Max an extra bottle from his pack. Max took a swig and then squirted some water on Jesse, laughing. Jesse calmly wiped his face with his shirt and kept walking.

"Check out the size of this thing!" Max yelled. He was the first to spot the huge redwood tree blackened by lightning. Both boys stood at the base of the trunk, staring up.

"I don't think I can even see the top!" whispered Jesse.

Then the boys noticed that fire had carved out a large hollow space at the base of the trunk. They stooped to step through the opening. Inside the hole, they could barely see each other in the darkness.

Max grinned as he ran his hand down the rough interior bark. "We're inside a tree!" he exclaimed. "I admit it—this is way better than watching a ballgame!"

1. Which part of the setting excited Max?
   - ● the inside of the redwood tree
   - Ⓑ the shaded path
   - Ⓒ the damp soil
   - Ⓓ the car he and Jesse rode in

2. How does Max show that he is unhappy?
   - Ⓐ He touches the inside of the redwood tree.
   - Ⓑ He complains during the hike.
   - Ⓒ He yells at Jesse.
   - Ⓓ He walks down the path.

3. Which of these is true about Jesse?
   - Ⓐ He is loud and lively.
   - Ⓑ He is clumsy and careless.
   - ● He is calm and quiet.
   - Ⓓ He is slow and angry.

4. Which adjective best describes the setting?
   - ● peaceful
   - Ⓑ dangerous
   - Ⓒ noisy
   - Ⓓ boring

Vo·cab·u·lar·y

A blended word combines two words into one. It usually begins with letters from one word and ends with letters from another. The first and second words' meanings combine to form the blended word's meaning.

gleam + shimmer = glimmer
The diamonds glimmer in the light.

Write the correct blended word from the box next to each equation below.

motel	smog	flurry	webcam
chortle	snazzy	clump	infomercial
videographer	fantabulous	emoticon	guesstimate

1. chunk + lump = __clump__
2. snappy + jazzy = __snazzy__
3. chuckle + snort = __chortle__
4. smoke + fog = __smog__
5. guess + estimate = __guesstimate__
6. video + photographer = __videographer__
7. flutter + hurry = __flurry__
8. fantastic + fabulous = __fantabulous__
9. emotion + icon = __emoticon__
10. motor + hotel = __motel__
11. information + commercial = __infomercial__
12. World Wide Web + camera = __webcam__

LANGUAGE LINES

Synonyms are two words that mean almost the same thing.

Choose the synonym in parentheses that best completes each sentence. Write the word on the line.

1. Maddy __gazed__ longingly at the new baseball glove in the store. (gazed, watched)
2. This weekend was her chance to show what an __excellent__ player she was. (enjoyable, excellent)
3. Maddy had practiced her __pitching__ every day after school. (pitching, tossing)
4. She was getting better and better at __catching__ the ball, too. (capturing, catching)
5. Maddy was __confident__ in herself, but she was still nervous. (certain, confident)
6. She knew that the __new__ mitt was just what she needed. (new, unused)
7. Maddy would __ask__ her mother tonight if she could buy it. (demand, ask)

In My Own Words

Your parents say you can go to camp this summer! Which type of camp would you choose—sports camp, computer camp, music camp, or another type? What would you hope to do there?

Sample answer:
   I would go to science camp. I would like to study the stars and look through a real telescope. I'd also like to find out more about plants and collect specimens to use for experiments.

Page 114

Mind Jigglers

Pizza Time

Three pizzas have been ordered for a pizza party. Each pizza has 10 slices. Each of the 15 guests gets 2 slices of pizza. Your job is to make sure that each guest gets 2 slices of pizza that he or she likes. You may give a guest 2 slices of the same pizza or of 2 different pizzas. Use numbers to show what kinds of pizza the guests will get. When you are done, every slice should be assigned to a guest. The first one has been done for you.

Pizza 1: Veggie Delight — Pizza 2: Pepperoni — Pizza 3: Ham and Pineapple

Sample answers:

Cassie will eat anything. 1 and 2	**Lila** is allergic to pepperoni. 1 and 3	**Jarid** is allergic to pineapple. 1 and 2
Kelly wants a lot of meat. 2 and 3	**Amber** does not like pepperoni. 1 and 3	**Olivia** likes pineapple and pepperoni. 2 and 3
Joshua loves pepperoni. 2 and 2	**Marcus** loves pepperoni. 2 and 2	**Chandra** likes ham but not pepperoni. 3 and 3
Micah does not eat ham. 1 and 2	**Solomon** does not like pepperoni. 1 and 3	**Benjamin** wants ham and pineapple. 3 and 3
Lucy loves vegetables. 1 and 1	**David** is a vegetarian. 1 and 1	**Tina** does not like vegetables. 2 and 3

114 Thursday

Page 115

MATH TIME

Data Sets

Use the rules below to help you complete the table.

To find the **range**, subtract the smallest number in a data set from the largest.

Data set: 3, 4, 5
5 − 3 = 2
The range is 2.

If all the numbers in the set are the same, there is no range.

To find the **mean**, add all of the numbers in the set and divide by the number of items in the set.

Data set: 3, 5, 7
3 + 5 + 7 = 15
15 ÷ 3 = 5
The mean is 5.

To find the **median**, list the numbers in order from least to greatest. The middle number is the median.

Data set: 3, 5, 7
The median is 5.

If there is an even amount of numbers in the set, add the two numbers in the middle and divide their sum in half.

The number in a set that appears the most often is the **mode**.

3, 5, 7, 5, 9
The mode is 5.

If no number appears more than once, there is no mode.

Data Set	Range	Mean	Median	Mode
10, 14, 15, 15, 17	7	14.2	15	15
3, 4, 6, 7, 7, 7, 8	5	6	7	7
21, 21, 21, 21, 21	no range	21	21	21
30, 35, 40, 45, 50	20	40	40	no mode
4, 5, 7, 9, 10, 10	6	7.5	8	10

Friday WEEK 9 115

Page 116

Geography

Regions of the United States

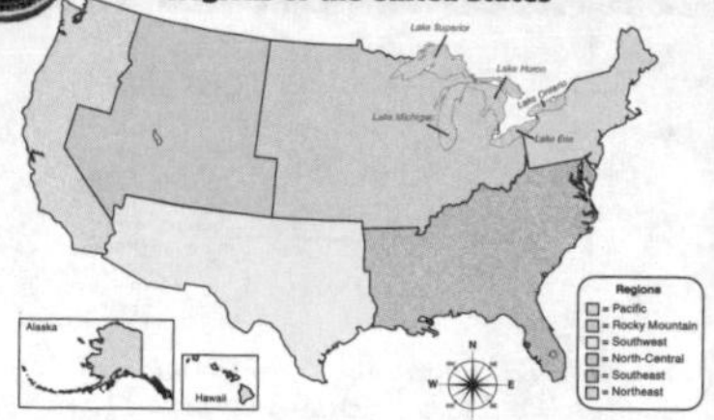

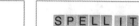

Use the map to answer the questions.

1. The United States is divided into how many regions? six
2. Which region is named for a major landform? Rocky Mountain
3. Alaska and Hawaii are part of which region? Pacific
4. Which region borders Lake Ontario? Northeast
5. Which region is farthest west? Pacific
6. In which region is Lake Superior? North-Central
7. Which region is between the Pacific region and the Southeast region? Southwest

116 Friday

Week 10

Page 119

Read It! Fiction

Read the story. Then answer the questions.

The Brave Pioneer

I'm a smart and brave pioneer. At least that's what I thought when my family and I set out for our long trip west on the Oregon Trail. But then I learned otherwise.

On the first night on the trail, Ma and my sisters slept in the wagon. I slept next to the fire with Pa. But just as I dropped off to sleep, a cricket crawled across my forehead. I didn't sleep at all for the rest of the night.

"We slept fine in the wagon," said my sister in the morning.

I thought I was smart and brave, so on the second night, I slept outside again but wore my hat. Just as I dropped off to sleep, a mouse tickled my big toe. I didn't sleep at all for the rest of the night.

"We slept fine in the wagon," said my sister in the morning.

I thought I was smart and brave, so on the third night, I slept outside again but wore my boots. Just as I dropped off to sleep, a snake slithered across my hand. I didn't sleep at all for the rest of the night.

"We slept fine in the wagon," said my sister in the morning.

I thought I was smart and brave, so on the fourth night, I slept outside again but wore my gloves. Not a single creature touched my skin. But I was so hot that I didn't sleep at all that night. In the morning, I decided I'd rather be smart and well-rested than brave and tired.

"Don't worry, son," said Pa. "You'll have plenty of chances to be brave on this trip." Then he pointed to the map. "See? There are no bridges across any of these rivers."

1. **Where will the boy in the story most likely sleep on the fifth night?**
   - ● in the wagon
   - Ⓑ closer to the fire
   - Ⓒ on top of his blankets
   - Ⓓ in a puddle
2. **How did the boy probably feel on the morning after the fourth night?**
   - ● tired
   - Ⓑ brave
   - Ⓒ smart
   - Ⓓ cold
3. **If the boy had felt a tickle on his neck, he probably would have ______**
   - Ⓐ slept closer to the fire
   - ● worn a scarf to bed
   - Ⓒ gotten up and run
   - Ⓓ woken his sister
4. **How will the boy be able to prove his bravery later in the story?**
   - Ⓐ by sleeping inside
   - Ⓑ by building a house
   - ● by crossing a river without a bridge
   - Ⓓ by guarding his mother and sisters

Monday WEEK 10 119

Page 120

Write It Right

Rewrite the letter and correct the errors.

june 3 2012

dear uncle roberto

thank you so much four the birthday present ive wnted my own guitar for ages and the won you baught me is purfict youre the best

love
pedro

June 3, 2012
Dear Uncle Roberto,
Thank you so much for the birthday present. I've wanted my own guitar for ages, and the one you bought me is perfect. You're the best!
Love,
Pedro

MATH TIME

Solve the problem below.

The school cafeteria offers the following menu each day. If a student picks one item from each category, how many different combinations can he order? 18

Choices for main dish:	Choices for side dish:	Choices for dessert:
• peanut butter-and-jelly sandwich • burrito • fish sticks	• vegetables • potatoes	• ice cream • brownie • cookies

120 Monday

Page 121

SPELL IT

Fill in the missing syllables to make the spelling words for the week. Then count the number of syllables in each word and write the number in the box.

1. en vi ron ment [4]
2. agri cul ture [4]
3. cur rency [3]
4. char acter is tic [5]
5. mu si cian [3]
6. sem icir cle [4]
7. in ter sec tion [4]
8. repre sen ta tive [5]
9. sub stitute [3]
10. civ iliza tion [5]
11. atmos phere [3]
12. am phib ian [4]

In My Own Words

Make up a new word. What does it mean? Use your new word in at least two sentences.

Sample answer:
bumbletastic: in a hugely embarrassing, awkward, or clumsy way

The way that the wide receiver dropped the pass and then fell into the crowd was bumbletastic.

I made the bumbletastic mistake of accidentally telling Dad about his surprise birthday party.

Tuesday WEEK 10 121

Page 122

LANGUAGE LINES

Antonyms are words that have opposite meanings.

Use the words from the box to complete the sentences with antonyms of the boldfaced words.

frequently neither similar scorching despises

1. My friend Benny **adores** baseball, but he despises football.
2. I **rarely** watch baseball, but I frequently watch football.
3. I like to be outside in **frigid** weather, and Benny likes to be outside when it's scorching.
4. Benny and I can be **opposite** in our tastes, but in other ways we're similar.
5. **Both** of us love basketball, and neither of us likes skating.

MATH TIME

Complete the multiple-choice questions about each grid below.

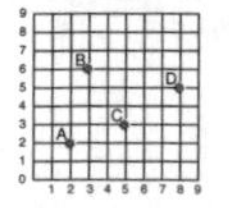

1. Which point is located at (3, 6)?
   ○ point A ○ point C
   ● point B ○ point D
2. Which point is located at (5, 3)?
   ○ point A ● point C
   ○ point B ○ point D
3. Which point is located at (2, 2)?
   ● point A ○ point C
   ○ point B ○ point D

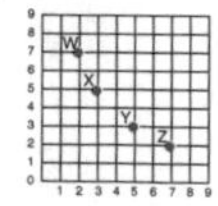

1. What is the ordered pair for point W?
   ● (2, 7) ○ (3, 5)
   ○ (7, 2) ○ (5, 3)
2. What is the ordered pair for point Z?
   ○ (2, 7) ○ (3, 5)
   ● (7, 2) ○ (5, 3)
3. What is the ordered pair for point Y?
   ○ (2, 7) ● (5, 3)
   ○ (7, 2) ○ (3, 5)

122 Tuesday

Page 123

Read It! Nonfiction

Read the article. Then answer the questions.

Creepy or Tasty?

How would you like to munch on a fat, pale caterpillar called a witchetty grub? Would you enjoy eating a delicious ant-egg taco? How does a wasp cracker sound to you? Caterpillars, ant eggs, and wasps are just three of the 1,500 different kinds of insects that are eaten by people around the world.

Here in the United States, most people are turned off by the thought of eating insects. But about 80 percent of people in the rest of the world include insects in their diet. Eating insects is not a bad idea. Insects are not only cheap, but they're also good for you. They have a lot of protein, vitamins, and minerals, and they have little fat.

People have different ways of preparing insect dishes. Sometimes the bugs are ground into flour and baked into cookies. Other times they are fried, roasted, boiled, or eaten raw. Depending on how the insects are prepared, their texture may be gooey, chewy, crunchy, or tender.

Their flavors can be compared to common foods that even Americans find delicious. For example, witchetty grubs are said to taste like almonds, chicken, or shrimp. Giant red ants, which people eat in Thailand, may taste like bacon. Some Australians enjoy the sweet taste of honeypot ants. And some people compare deep-fried bees to sunflower seeds, shrimp, or walnuts. It's all just a matter of taste!

1. **Which food has a taste similar to the taste of two insects mentioned in the passage?**
   - Ⓐ bacon
   - ● nuts
   - Ⓒ crackers
   - Ⓓ honey
2. **Which of these statements would the author probably agree with?**
   - Ⓐ It is hard to find insects to eat.
   - ● People should not be afraid to eat insects.
   - Ⓒ Americans are smart not to eat insects.
   - Ⓓ It is cruel to eat insects.
3. **Which statement is supported by details in the passage?**
   - Ⓐ Insects are hard to cook.
   - Ⓑ There is a right way and a wrong way to eat insects.
   - Ⓒ Grubs taste better than ants.
   - ● Insects are better for you than some other foods.
4. **Which insects might someone who likes shrimp be willing to try?**
   - Ⓐ witchetty grubs and red ants
   - Ⓑ honeypot ants and crickets
   - ● witchetty grubs and bees
   - Ⓓ honeypot ants and bees

Wednesday WEEK 10 123

Page 124

Vo·cab·u·lar·y

A **suffix** is a word part that comes after a base word or root.
A suffix changes a word's meaning and part of speech.

The suffixes **-able** and **-ible** form adjectives meaning "likely to," "can be," or "worthy of."
predict + able = **predictable** ("can be predicted")
reverse + ible = **reversible** ("can be reversed")

The suffixes **-ious** and **-ous** form adjectives meaning "full of" or "possessing the qualities of."
grace + ious = **gracious** ("full of grace")
venom + ous = **venomous** ("full of venom")

Answer each clue with a word that uses one of the suffixes above. If necessary, use a dictionary to help with spelling changes.

1. likely to be **adored** — a d o r a b l e
2. full of **glamour** — g l a m o r o u s
3. can be **avoided** — a v o i d a b l e
4. full of **fury** — f u r i o u s
5. full of **danger** — d a n g e r o u s
6. can be **accessed** — a c c e s s i b l e
7. full of **anxiety** — a n x i o u s
8. can be **depended** upon — d e p e n d a b l e
9. making good **sense** — s e n s i b l e
10. can be **chewed** — c h e w a b l e
11. can be **collected** — c o l l e c t i b l e
12. worthy of **admiring** — a d m i r a b l e

124 Wednesday

Answer Key 139

LANGUAGE LINES

Homophones are words that sound alike but have different spellings and meanings.

A. Circle the correct homophone to match the meaning.

Meaning		Homophone
1. how heavy something is	(weight)	wait
2. to put down on paper	right	(write)
3. belonging to them	they're	(their)
4. to make a harsh sound	(groan)	grown
5. in this place	(here)	hear
6. a piece of wood	bored	(board)

B. Write a sentence for each of these homophones. **Sample answers:**

Through: We walked through the crowd together.

Threw: Jason threw the ball into the air.

In My Own Words

You have decided to volunteer to help your community. What would you choose to do? Why?

Sample answer:
I would volunteer to work at a nursing home or retirement community because I think that older people deserve respect and attention. I also think I could learn a lot from being around them.

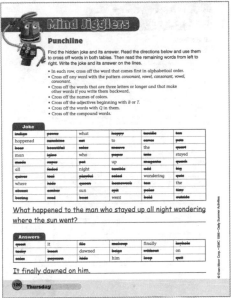

Mind Jigglers

Punchline

Find the hidden joke and its answer. Read the directions below and use them to cross off words in both tables. Then read the remaining words from left to right. Write the joke and its answer on the lines.

- In each row, cross off the word that comes first in alphabetical order.
- Cross off any word with the pattern *consonant, vowel, consonant, vowel, consonant.*
- Cross off the words that are three letters or longer and that make other words if you write them backward.
- Cross off the names of colors.
- Cross off the adjectives beginning with *B* or *T*.
- Cross off the words with *Q* in them.
- Cross off the compound words.

Joke

~~indigo~~	~~power~~	what	~~happy~~	~~terrible~~	ten
happened	~~sunshine~~	eat	to	~~seven~~	~~pots~~
~~bear~~	~~beautiful~~	~~soles~~	mauve	the	~~quart~~
man	~~igloo~~	who	~~paper~~	into	stayed
~~made~~	~~super~~	~~pot~~	up	~~magenta~~	~~queen~~
all	~~faded~~	night	~~terrible~~	add	~~big~~
~~quiver~~	~~tool~~	~~playful~~	~~salad~~	wondering	~~quit~~
where	~~hide~~	sun	~~spit~~	~~polar~~	the
~~absent~~	~~ember~~	~~homework~~	~~ten~~	~~tiny~~	
~~boring~~	~~read~~	~~boat~~	went	~~bold~~	~~outside~~

What happened to the man who stayed up all night wondering where the sun went?

Answers

~~quest~~	It	~~file~~	~~makeup~~	finally	~~keyhole~~
~~teaky~~	~~boast~~	dawned	~~beige~~	~~without~~	on
~~roses~~	~~popcorn~~	~~hide~~	him	~~keep~~	~~quit~~

It finally dawned on him.

MATH TIME

Mystery Shape

Draw a sketch of each of the following polygons using the clues given. Label the length of each side of the polygon. The first one has been done for you.

Remember:
- A right angle forms a square corner.
- An acute angle is less than a right angle.

Prime numbers can be divided only by 1 and themselves.
Congruent means having the same length and same angles.

1. This polygon has the following characteristics:
   - It has a perimeter of 12 inches.
   - It has four equal sides.
   - It has four right angles.

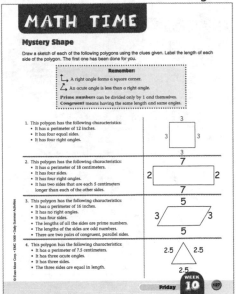

2. This polygon has the following characteristics:
   - It has a perimeter of 18 centimeters.
   - It has four sides.
   - It has four right angles.
   - It has two sides that are each 5 centimeters longer than each of the other sides.

3. This polygon has the following characteristics:
   - It has a perimeter of 16 inches.
   - It has no right angles.
   - It has four sides.
   - The lengths of all the sides are prime numbers.
   - The lengths of the sides are odd numbers.
   - There are two pairs of congruent, parallel sides.

4. This polygon has the following characteristics:
   - It has a perimeter of 7.5 centimeters.
   - It has three acute angles.
   - It has three sides.
   - The three sides are equal in length.

Geography

Central America

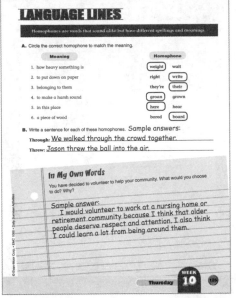

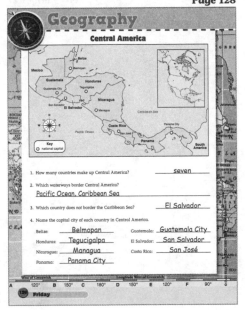

1. How many countries make up Central America? **seven**

2. Which waterways border Central America?
   Pacific Ocean, Caribbean Sea

3. Which country does not border the Caribbean Sea? **El Salvador**

4. Name the capital city of each country in Central America.

Belize:	Belmopan	Guatemala:	Guatemala City
Honduras:	Tegucigalpa	El Salvador:	San Salvador
Nicaragua:	Managua	Costa Rica:	San José
Panama:	Panama City		

summer journal

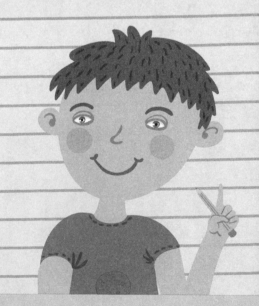